W9-CRM-410

CAMBRIDGE TEXTS IN THE
HISTORY OF POLITICAL THOUGHT

Luther and Calvin on Secular Authority

CAMBRIDGE TEXTS IN THE HISTORY OF POLITICAL THOUGHT

Series editors

RAYMOND GEUSS *Colombia University*
QUENTIN SKINNER *Christ's College, Cambridge*

The series is intended to make available to students the most important texts required for an understanding of the history of political thought. The scholarship of the present generation has greatly expanded our sense of the range of authors indispensable for such an understanding, and the series will reflect those developments. It will also include a number of less well-known works, in particular those needed to establish the intellectual contexts that in turn help to make sense of the major texts. The principal aim, however, will be to produce new versions of the major texts themselves, based on the most up-to-date scholarship., The preference will always be for complete texts, and a special feature of the series will be to complement individual texts, within the compass of a single volume, with subsidiary contextual material. Each volume will contain an introduction on the historical identity and contemporary significance of the work or works concerned, as well as a chronology, notes on further reading and (where appropriate) brief biographical sketches of significant individuals mentioned in each text.

For a list of titles published in the series, please see end of book

CAMBRIDGE TEXTS IN THE
HISTORY OF POLITICAL THOUGHT

Luther and Calvin on Secular Authority

EDITED AND TRANSLATED
BY HARRO HÖPFL

Senior Lecturer, Lancaster University

CAMBRIDGE
UNIVERSITY PRESS

Published by the Press Syndicate of the University of Cambridge
The Pitt Building, Trumpington Street, Cambridge CB2 1RP
40 West 20th Street, New York, NY 10011–4211, USA
10 Stamford Road, Oakleigh, Melbourne 3166, Australia

First published 1991
Reprinted 1993

Printed in Great Britain by J. W. Arrowsmith Ltd, Bristol

British Library cataloguing in publication data
Luther and Calvin on secular authority. – (Cambridge texts
in the history of political thought).
1. Politics.   Theories of Luther, Martin, 1843–1546   2.
Politics. Theories of Calvin, Jean, 1509–1564
I. Höpfl, Harro *1943*–
320.5

Library of Congress cataloguing in publication data
Luther and Calvin on secular authority / edited and translated by
Harro Höpfl.
p.   cm. – (Cambridge texts in the history of political
thought)
Includes index.
Translation of: Von weltlicher Oberkeit and De politica
administratione, bk. 4, ch. 20 of Institutio Christianae religionis.
Contents: On secular authority – On civil government.
ISBN 0-521-34208-2. – ISBN 0-521-34986-9 (pbk.)
1. Church and state – Lutheran Church – Early works to 1800.
2. Church and state – Reformed Church – Early works to 1800.
3. Lutheran Church – Doctrines – Early works to 1800.   4. Reformed
Church – Doctrines – Early works to 1800.   1. Höpfl, Harro.
II. Luther, Martin, 1483–1546. Von weltlicher Oberkeit. English.
1991.   III. Calvin, Jean, 1509–1564. Institutio Christianae Religionis,
Ch.20: De politica administratione.
English.   1991.   IV. Series.
BV629.L8   1991
261.7–dc20   90–38346   CIP

ISBN 0 521 34208 2 hardback
ISBN 0 521 34986 9 paperback

BS

Contents

Acknowledgements

Richard Tuck, Quentin Skinner and Raymond Geuss all offered encouragement and tried to impose some shape on the form and content of the book, especially the introductory material and the footnotes. Christine Lyall Grant had the herculean labour of standardizing the format of a recalcitrant text. And my colleague Russell Price once again placed at my disposal his remarkable ability to see what is actually on the printed page, as opposed to what I imagined was there. He also demanded, and usually got, a large number of clarifications. To all of them my most grateful thanks, even if (probably unwisely) I did not always follow their advice. The book is dedicated to HJH (to make up for the fact that it's not only when translating that I can't always find the right words), and to MH and GWA, because they too should have a dedication.

Introduction

The movement for religious reform and regeneration which attained self-definition and organization from about 1520 onwards – in the next century it came to be called 'The Reformation' – engaged the attention of princes and magistrates from the very beginning, whether as patrons, beneficiaries or opponents. For their part, the spokesmen and prime movers of reformation, usually clerics subject to ecclesiastical discipline from which only secular rulers could shield them, habitually sought to enlist rulers in their cause, particularly when the papacy and a part of the clergy proved obdurate. Secular rulers had been involved more or less officially in the administration, finances, staffing and even the doctrine of the Church since the late Roman Empire. Conversely, ecclesiastics doubled as secular potentates or were members of a 'Church' which, humanly speaking, was a polity with its own rulers, laws, courts and subjects, as well as its own taxes and property. Such was the interpenetration of secular and spiritual in the sixteenth century that no reformation of religion could take place without a transformation of the public order of the commonwealths of Christian Europe, and no such transformation could be institutionalized without the assistance of secular rulers.

Martin Luther (1483–1546) was a former Augustinian monk and priest, and a lecturer at the University of Wittenberg. As an ecclesiastic, and especially after his excommunication by the papacy in 1521, not only his freedom to work but his very life depended on the protection of secular rulers, notably the very cautious but nonetheless firm and loyal Frederick the Wise, Elector of Saxony, to whom Luther paid eloquent if oblique tribute in *On Secular Authority*. From the beginning of his career as a reformer, he had looked to secular rulers to initiate or consolidate reformation. In 1520 he addressed one of his seminal pamphlets *To the Christian Nobility of the German Nation*. In it he sought to persuade the Emperor and the princes of Germany to use their authority to eliminate the ill-gotten wealth, temporal power and chicaneries of the papacy and the higher clergy, to see to the summoning of a Council of the Church, to ensure a married, preaching and resident parish clergy, to reform the theology and philosophy curricula of the universities (where clerics were educated), and to institute a drastic limitation on the number and size of the religious orders. In all this they were not to be frightened or side-tracked by the raging and anathemas of Rome, or the monopoly of teaching authority claimed by the 'spiritual estate': every Christian is a member of the 'spiritual estate' in this regard, entitled to judge doctrine for himself. In a word, what confronted Christians was the 'tyranny' of the Roman Church. Any Christian ought to do what he could to overturn this tyranny, but secular rulers were more advantageously placed than others to act effectively.

Luther's strategy for reformation was not at all distinctive. The reformers originally intended, and continued to intend, the reformation of the whole of Christendom. They soon found, however, that such comprehensiveness was impracticable in the foreseeable future. Thenceforth the Reformation took divergent paths. The 'Radical Reformation' is a term commonly used to refer to those who either sought the take-over of secular authority by the self-selecting members (or leaders) of churches composed exclusively of 'the Elect', or more usually withdrew from contact with secular authority as far as possible, and formed themselves into voluntary and exclusive (although proselytizing) congregations. This course of action frequently brought them persecution at the hands of the secular authorities. The 'Magistral' (or 'Magisterial') Reformers, on the other hand, who included Luther and Calvin, aimed at, or found themselves committed to, a reformation limited to particular territories subject to the jurisdiction of some secular ruler or magistracy not implacably opposed to 'the Gospel'. All the inhabitants of these territories, once reformation had been made official by their rulers, were expected to foreswear 'popery' and subscribe to evangelical religion as a condition of residence. These inhabitants were described as composing the 'Church' of that particular territory, or *Land*, the *Landeskirche*. The price for the cooperation of secular authorities in declaring reformation official, and implementing the changes in the public order that it required, was entitlement to intervene in the appointment of the clergy (and the related profession of teachers) and usually surveillance of every aspect of the life of 'their' *Landeskirchen*. A reformation in this manner, however limited and unsatisfactory, at least guaranteed some approximation to the inclusiveness of the Old Church and protected against disorderly (and even violent and millennialist) proceedings and sectarianism.

A strategy of enlisting the cooperation of sympathetic secular rulers was obvious enough, but ecclesiastical independence, however compromised in practice, soon proved to be something which was not to be thrown away casually. Indeed, all the reformers who took this course soon learnt what indeed they might have anticipated, namely that the favour of princes is fitful and unreliable, and never comes without strings. More immediately pressing, however, was the fact that some rulers proved hostile to reformation. In *On Secular Authority* Luther named some of them, but he left the most important one unidentified: the Holy Roman Emperor Charles V, whom he had known to be his implacable opponent from the Reichstag at Worms in 1521 onwards. Luther's first response to such hostility was to assert complete autonomy for the Church, a position as untenable as his earlier open invitation to princes to take the work of reformation in hand.

Luther: *On Secular Authority*

Luther had been meditating a book devoted to the rights and duties of secular rulers for some time when, on 7 November 1522, George Duke of Saxony issued an edict which prohibited the buying and selling of Luther's translation of the New Testament, and demanded the surrender, by Christmas, of all privately held copies, in exchange for the purchase price. This episode spurred Luther on to immediate and rapid composition: he was able to write the prefatory Letter to *On Secular Authority* by Christmas Day, 1522, and the book appeared in March 1523.

Most (though not all) of the main themes and organizing ideas that informed Luther's thought about the polity are to be found in this work. Nothing else from his pen comes even close to it in generality, specificity of concern with the polity, or coherence; hence its appearance here. Nevertheless, it can no more be taken as a digest of the whole of Luther's political thought than any other of his writings. Luther certainly brought to his political thinking the preoccupations of a highly sophisticated theology. But he also brought to it much else that may or may not have been coherent with that theology, but was certainly independent of it. Moreover, he was inclined to speak generally and abstractly, when his attention was in fact focussed on specific persons, occasions and issues. In 1522/3, he was mindful chiefly of rulers hostile to reformation. But when Luther's mind was on sympathetic princes and magistrates, or on the threats posed to the world and reformation alike by 'fanatics', 'prophets', 'murderous hordes of peasants' and suchlike, a quite different account of 'secular authority' made its appearance, an account which was equally general and abstract in form, but much more favourable and indulgent towards secular rulers. That attitude is not entirely absent even in *On Secular Authority*, which contains some of Luther's harshest generalizations about rulers.

On Secular Authority, then, shows Luther at his most hostile to secular authority: true religion is presented here as being more divorced from the life of the civil community than in any earlier or later account, as more private and more personal; a more restricted jurisdiction is assigned to rulers; and the true Church is portrayed as more independent of their authority. Conversely, we find Luther here offering a justification of religious toleration that squares neither with his later attitude to the repression of heresy and blasphemy, nor with a good part of the themes of his theology. And, finally, this text contains no intimation of the idea that public, political measures might be taken against an ungodly ruler.

Thus in *On Secular Authority* Luther represented the Church as a free congregation (*Gemeinde*, also meaning a community, parish or commune), in which every Christian is a 'King, Priest and Prophet'. This was not intended to deny the practical necessity of a distinct priestly office; indeed Luther was not even opposed to a reformed episcopacy. Rather his point was to assert the fundamental liberty and equality of all Christians, and to subject all hierarchies and earthly superiors to this fundamental liberty and equality. Hence also Luther's occasional displays of an inclination to allow to congregations a much greater say in the appointment and supervision of ministers, an inclination congruent with the idea (also nurtured in the 'Radical Reformation') of the Church as a free and voluntary congregation, tolerant of 'authorities' other than Scripture only to the extent that these are merely the appointed agents of the congregation. This theme in his thought proved evanescent; more usually he tolerated appointment and payment of pastors and teachers by magistrates and princes, which *de facto* was already the practice.

Such a vision of Christian equality and Christian liberty (the latter being an evangelical slogan and the title of Luther's most famous work) was clearly incompatible with the use of coercion, lawcourts and ordinary civil penalties and punishments as instruments of ecclesiastical order; hence Luther's insistence on the need to keep secular and spiritual 'government' distinct, despite the obvious practical impossibility of doing anything of the sort. By parity of reasoning it seems that the Church cannot be anything but a voluntary and indeed a private association. This latter implication Luther here accepted, albeit without appearing to realize that it entailed the denial of the idea that the Church should have a membership coextensive with that of some civil polity. This idea he merely took for granted, for his object was always to reform an existing Church, not to found a new one.

At this time Luther had not fully discerned the threat posed to the orthodox reformation and (as he came to see it) to the peace of the whole world by the sectarians' 'gathered' churches, composed exclusively of the Elect. The appeal of this idea of the true Church, so closely analogous to the persecuted, or at best tolerated, assemblies ('churches') of Christian believers of the New Testament, was one he found hard to resist. Conversely, he never gave any reason why civil subjection and membership of a particular Church should coincide.

On Secular Authority thus marshals the arguments which could be used to advocate religious toleration, and even the reconstitution of churches as private associations, and does it so cogently that Sébastien Châteillon (Castellio)[1] could simply reproduce this part of the book in his own plea for toleration. Luther was not of course adopting this position merely out of political expediency. On the contrary,

[1] Sébastien Châteillon, Castalio or Castellion (Castello), 1515–63, was an evangelical humanist who, after conversion, left France for Strasbourg in 1540 and was made head of the newly founded Academy of Geneva by Calvin the following year. Theological differences with Calvin obliged him to leave Geneva for Basle in 1544, where he remained until his death, writing (*inter alia*) a translation of the Bible in Latin and French. After the execution of the noted heretic Servetus in 1550, Châteillon, under the pseudonym Martinus Bellius, published *Whether Heretics are to be Persecuted*, 1554. See below, p. xxiv.

libertarian, egalitarian, communal motifs were part of the texture of his theology.

What holds Luther's political thought together is not unchanging doctrines or attitudes, but the continuing attempt to establish a congruence between his views of the polity and his (logically as well as chronologically) prior theology of the Christian and his relationship to God. In this attempt he employed a vocabulary, and the assumptions it incapsulated, which were highly derivative and conventional; there is nothing in Luther's political writings reminiscent of the genius for devising the appropriate concept, or of that relentless independence and thoroughness so characteristic of his theology. And the fact that he simply appropriated an extant vocabulary, rather than submitting its contents to inspection, led him into certain tangles, much as it did his contemporary, Machiavelli.

Let us begin with the title of the book: *Von Weltlicher Oberkeit.* *Weltlich* is a highly troublesome term, and not only for the translator. It is the adjective from *Welt*, the world, and thus means: secular, temporal, worldly, earthly. It had a well-established usage in distinguishing between the secular, or temporal, authorities of Christian commonwealths and the spiritual and ecclesiastical ones, and in this sense the term is neutral and merely designative. This is the principal sense of the term here: Luther's subject was secular authority and secular rulers, not popes, prelates and priests.

But the matter is not as simple as this. Terms derive part of their meaning from those to which they are usually counterposed, and part from the company they habitually keep. The standard antonyms for *weltlich* were terms with highly favourable connotations: heavenly, celestial, eternal, spiritual; conversely, 'the world' was commonly linked with 'the devil' and 'the flesh', not least in the works of St Augustine, Luther's and the Reformers' favourite patristic theologian. So although *weltlich* does have a neutral, merely designative sense ('secular' as opposed to 'ecclesiastical'), it wears the pejorative connotation of 'worldly', 'this-worldly' (which are the same word in German as 'secular') on its sleeve. Neither 'secular' nor 'temporal' quite capture this; both will serve equally well or badly.

Luther used this terminology in *On Secular Authority* to distinguish areas of jurisdiction and competence for 'secular' and 'spiritual' governors. The distinction is crucial to the implicit *non sequitur* in Luther's argument that because rulers are 'secular', they are to concern themselves only with secular matters. But on Luther's own understanding, religion is not a sphere of life, or a class of matters, things or concerns, but rather an aspect of every sphere of life, every matter, every thing or concern. Nevertheless, in Part II of *On Secular Authority* he attempts to safeguard religion against the unwelcome attentions of ungodly princes by trying to separate secular and spiritual *matters*, allocating them to their respective agencies. He does not of course ask exactly what is a *weltlich* matter, but then neither did his successors until the next century; he casually takes it that secular matters are matters concerned with the body, honour and property. Now, since bibles, Luther's proximate concern, were very much property (indeed the rulers confiscating them were scrupulous in refunding the purchase price, thus respecting their character as property), Luther was already in difficulty: not every item in the genus property is of the same kind, it seems. Exactly the same goes for secular peace, tranquillity, justice and so forth.

Luther saw the duty of secular governors, traditionally enough, as keeping the peace, enforcing conformity to laws, protecting the law-abiding and punishing law-breakers. But his language here also generates ambiguity. His term for the law-abiding is *die Frommen*, which in his vocabulary means: those who do their duty to God and men, and hence: the just or morally upright (cf. Glossary: just). But this term does not make the distinction Luther was careful to make elsewhere (e.g. in *On Good Works* of 1520) between 'outward' justice, mere conformity to rules, and 'true' or 'inward' justice, which is a quality of the intention. Similarly, Luther's term for law-breakers is simply 'the wicked' (*die Bösen*), or 'evil-doers' (*Übeltäter*). Thus what Luther actually says is that the duty of rulers is to protect the good and to coerce, inhibit and punish the wicked.

In the same way, he left vague the distinction between civil and moral law. At various points, he casually asserted that true Christians naturally obey 'the law'. This makes sense only on the assumption that *das Recht* (i.e. positive law, the law of the land; cf. Glossary: law) in fact ordains what is morally and spiritually right (*recht*). He then argues that Christians accordingly need neither laws (which must mean positive laws), nor anything that goes with the enforcement of laws. He furthermore infers from this that Christians are no threat to rulers, but rather a positive asset. In any case, the crucial component of a civil polity for Luther is not secular law at all, but rulers. Indeed at various points in

On Secular Authority he goes out of his way to voice the opinion, characteristic of early modern partisans of absolute monarchy, that a wise prince must have discretion to override the law, must indeed keep it as firmly in hand as the head of a household keeps under his discretion such rules as he has made for the disposition of the domestic order. What matters is rulers and ruling; it is these that constitute a polity.

The principal organizing idea in Luther's political thought is *Oberkeit* (cf. Glossary: authority). German-speakers of Luther's time would automatically have resorted to this now obsolete term to translate *potestas* (which Lonitzer, see p. xxiv, used in the title of his translation) or *auctoritas*, 'authority'. It is for this reason that the title of the book has here been rendered as 'On Secular Authority', which also follows the precedent set by other translators. But in fact the synonymity of *auctoritas / potestas* and *Oberkeit* is by no means perfect. At many points in the text it has been necessary to substitute 'superiors', 'those in (or with) authority (or power)', or even the infelicitous word 'superiority'. For, unlike 'authority', the German word cannot fail to call to mind the *persons* who are in authority, 'superiors' (*die Oberen*, also obsolete). And this property of the term sits well with the character of Luther's thought, for he tends to personalize political authority.

Luther thus conceives of the polity as a relationship between superiors and inferiors, rulers and subjects, public and private persons. Unlike Calvin, he does not qualify this by any civic humanist notions of private persons as citizens (for Luther they are 'subjects'), or of rulers as generically 'magistrates'. Rulers are 'superiors', 'princes' (*Fürsten*) and 'lords and masters' (*Herren*). The emphasis, implicit in the very terminology Luther employs, is throughout on the right to command, the duty to obey, and the mastery over resources to ensure compliance with commands. The completion of this circle would be to treat law itself as a species of command; it is not, however, clear that Luther took this step. And because he did not equate the law of the Holy Roman Empire with the will of Holy Roman Emperors, he was able in the 1530s to assert a legal right of godly princes subject to the Holy Roman Emperor to resist the Emperor when he acted outside his constitutional authority. Calvin and his followers were to take exactly the same line with the French kings (or regents) and the *anciennes loix* of France, a line of argument already implicit in the *Institution* (p. xviii below). But in *On Secular Authority* Luther gets nowhere near this; the rigorously a- or anti-political ethic of New Testament Christianity can find no relationship of the Christian to the polity other than an in-but-not-of-the-polity quiescence, service to rulers in the things which are Caesar's, or prayer and suffering ('passive resistance'); this is the manner of conducting themselves towards tyrants consistently enjoined upon private persons by both Luther and Calvin.

What secular authority (in other words, rulers and their power) is put into the world to do, as far as Luther is concerned, is to prevent chaos, given the overwhelming preponderance of the ungodly and the Un-christian in the world. This cannot be done by laws alone, or by law-making: the point is not to make new laws, but to enforce existing ones. The crucial term here is *Gewalt*, which, according to the Grimms' *Deutsches Wörterbuch*, means any or all of: power, strength, might, efficacy . . . empire, rule, dominion, mastery, sway, jurisdiction, government, protection . . . *potestas, facultas, imperium, dictio, arbitrium, ius* . . . *potentia, vis, violentia, iniuria, indignitas*. Its most prominent meaning, however, is force, power or might. In many passages in *On Secular Authority* Luther uses the term interchangeably with *Oberkeit*; he might indeed have used it for the title of the work. But what *potestas* would conceal, and *Oberkeit* partly conceals, is that *Gewalt* can mean – and often in the text does mean – mere coercion, force, or violence. For what is crucial, given Luther's Augustinian cast of thought, is not that power should be exercised legitimately and by duly authorized office-holders (*potestates*), but that someone should use force (*Gewalt*) to prevent the ungodly from tearing each other to pieces, even if those who use such force are no better than those against whom they use it. God's will and purposes are served whether rulers act from benevolent or wicked motives. 'Frogs need storks.' Nor was the distinction (of which Luther was of course perfectly well aware) between an office and its occupant of any consequence: it is enough for Christians to know that power itself is of divine ordinance, and provided rulers do not use their power to 'hurl souls into hell', one person will do as well as another for a ruler. Calvin took much the same view. Thus Luther's original (1522) translation of the crucial scriptural passage Romans 13.1–3 – much of Protestant political thought may be read, and indeed presented itself, as a commentary on this text – was: 'Let everyone be subject to the *Oberkeit* and power (*Gewalt*), for there is no power (*Gewalt*) but from God. But the power (*Gewalt*) which is in every place [this seems to mean: whatever *Gewalt* is to be found anywhere] . . .' The

1544 version, however, reads: 'Let every person be subject to the *Oberkeit*, which has power (*Gewalt*) over him. For there is no *Oberkeit* but from God. But wherever there is *Oberkeit* . . .' The version Luther offered in *On Secular Authority* is almost identical to the 1522 text. Thus it seems that there was a distinction for Luther between *Gewalt* and *Oberkeit*; although he could use them interchangeably, the latter had more of a connotation of legitimacy, the former of force. In 1523 the distinction was a matter of indifference to him, but it was force and coercion he was concerned to stress.

It is in this connection that 'the sword' should be mentioned. For Luther this is the symbol, emblem and substance of secular authority. This was conventional enough. And of course there is a Christian tradition of embroidering on certain biblical texts which mention the 'sword'. Most of these are prominently displayed in Luther's text; some are conspicuous by their absence in both Luther and Calvin; e.g. Matthew 26.52; Isaiah 2.4 (a favourite with the 'Radical Reformation' in its quietistic phase); Luke 22.38. But however conventional the usage, metaphors are never innocent, and there is no doubt that Luther meant the 'sword' reference most literally; it is not the Judge, but the Executioner who epitomizes ruling for Luther.

Calvin: *Institution of the Christian Religion*

Jean Calvin (1509–64), a former student of law and already the author of a commentary on Seneca's *On Clemency*, was obliged to flee his native France for Basle in 1534 because of his evangelical convictions. In 1536 he published the first (Latin) edition of his *Institution of the Christian Religion*. The book was an immediate success. Luther himself welcomed it, and it is clear from the book itself that Calvin's conversion had taken place under Lutheran auspices. There is, however, no unequivocal evidence that Calvin had ever read *On Secular Authority* (see p. xxiv below). The part of the book that is offered in translation here began life in that edition as the concluding section of the final chapter: 'On Christian Liberty, Ecclesiastical Authority (*potestas*), and Civil Government (*administratio*)'.

The linking of these three themes and the choice of 'civil government' for the peroration of the book were signs of the times. So is the *Epistle Dedicatory*, addressed to the then king of France, François I, but retained in the editions subsequent to his death. In that Epistle Calvin assured the addressee (and with him all rulers) of the orthodoxy, piety and political dutifulness of his Protestant subjects. The rest of the book scrupulously avoided anything connected with the polity, until the last chapter. There, the main point Calvin was concerned to convey about the bedrock evangelical doctrine of Christian liberty was that it was entirely compatible with the most perfect submission to temporal authority. Obedience is also the dominant theme of the last section, 'On Civil Government'. For, although the very last paragraph of the section, and therefore of the whole book, exhorts Christians to 'obey God rather than men', the rest had been at pains to stress the Christian duty of obedience to rulers, irrespective of the quality of their titles, their conduct or their religion. If disobedience to ungodly commands becomes inevitable, it must take the form of prayer, supplication, suffering or exile, but not rebellion.

Calvin was a second-generation reformer. He began work only when reformed religion was already dividing into denominations, sometimes bitterly hostile to each other; during his career the Romanists were beginning to put their house in order and the Council of Trent finished its deliberations in 1563. The military fortunes of the German Protestants were at a low ebb in the 1540s, and in France the kings became as hostile to the 'new religion' as the Emperor Charles V. To compound these difficulties, Romanists delighted in tarring the Magistral Reformers with the brush of anabaptism; and sectarians, indeed, continued to dog every step of the orthodox reformers. Shortly before Calvin composed the first *Institution*, a horrified Christendom had seen the rise and apocalypse of an anabaptist venture in millenial rule at Münster (1533–5), an insurrection terminated only by the combined forces of Catholic and Protestant princes, and with exemplary savagery. Peasant wars, religious wars and civil upheavals were all alike blamed by the papists on 'the Fifth Gospel', which had originated in Luther's satanic pride and insubmission (however euphemized into the doctrine of Christian Liberty) and which was now bearing fruit according to the character of the tree.

These charges were hard to rebut. By this time, the German Lutherans (with Luther's somewhat reluctant assent) had indeed devised a justification for resisting their supreme overlord the Emperor both politically and militarily. Equally, the Reformers had become anxious to restore some element of clerical independence. But reformed religion was now, if anything, more acutely dependent than ever on the protection of rulers against Romanists without and sectarians within.

In the circumstances, insistence on the duty of political obedience was imperative, but equally any statement of that duty had to be a qualified one. Calvin's original strategy, as a reading of the text which brackets out the post-1536 additions makes clear, closely resembled that of Luther's in 1523. On the one hand, he inculcated an (if anything) even more extreme doctrine of political obedience and passivity; on the other, he tried to safeguard true religion by means of Luther's distinction between the jurisdictions of secular and spiritual governments, allotting to rulers charge over a 'merely external' righteousness, while leaving true piety and religion to God and an unspecified 'Church'. And Calvin's 1536 discussion of the Church confined itself almost exclusively to a congenial and conventional assault upon the 'tyranny' of the Romanists, instead of broaching the divisive and intractable matter of the public order of a reformed Church.

In one passage, Calvin went further and cautiously advanced the doctrine devised by Lutherans to justify war against the Emperor: if a civil order of laws and institutions (a *politia/police*) provides for them, 'popular magistrates' may collectively resist 'tyrants'. Lutherans had said 'lesser magistrates'. Calvin hazarded the view that modern Estates General, *Reichstage* or Parliaments may be institutions of this sort, corresponding to Spartan Ephors and Roman Tribunes of the People. Here he was relying on the distinction between *public* persons, for whom political action was legitimate and indeed a duty, and *private* persons, to whom the doctrine of 'passive obedience' (a significant sixteenth-century euphemism, which clearly meant passive *dis*obedience) continued to apply with undiminished rigour. 'Popular magistrates' are *public* persons. In his later work, Calvin added nothing more to the doctrine of resistance; the momentous developments it received in Calvinist circles are the work of his followers in France, Holland and elsewhere. However, the interpretation of 'tyranny' and of what was the actual *police* of (for example) France, left a great deal of latitude. Calvin's growing antipathy to monarchy also left its mark on the *Institution*.

But despite his conventionally Lutheran distinctions between Christian liberty and civil obedience, true and external justice, spiritual and civil governments, Calvin also from the first allotted to magistrates the policing of 'idolatry', 'sacrilege', 'blasphemy', and other public affronts to religion (in other words popery and anabaptism); this was by then also Luther's doctrine. Equally, he was careful to distinguish between popish, tyrannical impositions, and just and acceptable laws necessary for the good order of the Church, as for any other human association, and to be enforced by rulers.

Changes in Calvin's thinking are first manifested in the second edition of the *Institution* of 1539, the (first) French translation of 1541, and in the most fundamental revision of all for our purposes, the (Latin) edition of 1543. By this time Calvin, in company with others, had reformed and reorganized the Church in Geneva, until his expulsion in 1538; had had first-hand experience at Strasbourg of sympathetic magistrates, of a well-ordered Church in a free city, and of the diplomacy, ecclesiastical and civil, of the reformed polities with each other and with the Romanists; he had been restored in late 1541 as leading 'pastor' of Geneva and had been able to implement the main lines of a reformed Church there, with the sometimes reluctant but indispensable cooperation of the magistracy. The rest of his life was spent in Geneva, participating in its ecclesiastical and civil life, consolidating its reformation and specifically the authority of the 'Venerable Company of Pastors', a collegially organized clerical body charged with governing Geneva in its spiritual and ecclesiastical aspects. All this, in Calvin's interpretation of the lessons to be learned, left its mark on the *Institution* and in his voluminous scriptural commentaries. It should be borne in mind that when he wrote the first edition of the *Institution*, he had no experience of managing church affairs; unlike the first generation of Reformers, he had not even been a priest in the Old Church. Some of the salient changes appear as alterations to the text of the first edition; some others cannot be found in the passages translated here and are therefore briefly rehearsed below.

Thus from the *Institution* of 1541 onwards, the 'invisible' Church composed exclusively of the Elect almost completely recedes from view. All Calvin's interest now came to centre on the 'visible' Church, its organization, authority and activities. The original last chapter was broken up into three separate chapters; a discussion of the concrete organizational features of 'visible' Churches was added. The 'political' chapter (which is what the original section 'On political *administratio*' had now become) ceased to be the last chapter. But in the last edition of the book, the only one with whose structure Calvin professed himself satisfied, it again became the last chapter. Here the ecclesiological section was again part of the same 'book', Book IV: 'Of the Outward Means of Salvation', chs. 1–12. But Calvin's ecclesiology now encompassed a comprehensive account of what he deemed to be the scripturally ordained order of a true visible Church, as well as a greatly expanded anti-papist polemic, an activity to which he remained addicted.

The reformed Church, from 1543 onwards, is again seen to be 'governed' by a 'clergy' – Calvin did not hesitate to use such terms – with a degree of independence and authority. All the other Magistral Reformers had recognized by about 1530 that they had given far more to secular authority than they had ever intended. The recruitment of ecclesiastical personnel and the supervision of the doctrine, piety and morals of the congregation, so it was now generally believed, ought at least in some measure to be in the hands of a Reformed ministry, and not simply one of the things which secular rulers attended to, or neglected.

Any attempt to raise the standing, independence and power of the clergy was of course bound to meet with resistance from ostensibly evangelical rulers and congregations, all seasoned anticlericals. A clear distinction had therefore to be drawn between the 'tyranny' of popes and prelates, and the rightful authority of a godly company of Reformed pastors. In any case, it was a genuine concern of Calvin to avoid any recurrence of the corruption of the Gospel. He appears to have seen the avoidance of any semblance of monarchy as the principal organizational preservative against ecclesiastical tyranny. The alternative was a collegial, corporate ministry, permitting nothing more monarchical than a *primus inter pares*; speaking in the language of political theory, the best form for a Church (and more important, Calvin would have added, the form ordained by Scripture) is aristocracy or the mixed polity, compounded of aristocratic and democratic components. The more godly the congregation, the more reason for a democratic (or in ecclesiastical terms, congregational) component; there was, at any rate, no justification for stripping congregations of every vestige of authority in the supervision of the clergy. For, just as an aristocracy's individual members are to police each other, so aristocrats collectively need to be policed, just as subjects collectively need to be policed by the collectivity of rulers.

Such reasoning was of course equally applicable to the polity; indeed, a striking aspect of Calvin's ecclesiology is the extent to which it is suffused with political terminology; the whole of the doctrine of the mixed polity was derivable, and in fact derived from, classical and medieval political thought. But it was entirely idle for Calvin to specify the best (indeed the only scriptural, and therefore the only ultimately tolerable) order of the Church, if he did not at the same time reflect about how a civil polity might be ordered which would allow the instituting and functioning of such an ecclesiastical order. But certain difficulties stood in the way of a forthright formulation on Calvin's part of an inferential argument about the best structure of a polity.

Just as Luther inclined to the providentialist view that Romans 13 refers to whomever we find equipped with power, and that Christians have no business curiously inspecting the titles of those they find in authority, so did Calvin. In the 1536 *Institution* he had even denied that it was legitimate for private men to discuss amongst themselves what would be the best form of polity: God's decree establishes different forms in different places. But in subsequent editions, Calvin himself introduced (in section 8) an explicit if circumspect advocacy of the aristocratic or mixed form of polity. Thus the best form of civil polity precisely parallels the divinely ordained form of ecclesiastical polity. His hostility to monarchy also became more and more apparent, although it is to be found in the ecclesiological chapters of the *Institution* and in his scriptural commentaries, rather than in the political chapter. (A section from the first edition which had argued a divine predilection for monarchy, however, remained; it was not Calvin's way ever to retract anything he had written.) He also made clear that what he opposed was not political speculation as such, but seditious discussions on the part of private men.

What is more, he now virtually abandoned the attempt to distinguish an area of secular matters, over which secular rulers were to have jurisdiction, replacing it with a much more defensible distinction between the *means* employed by secular and spiritual governors respectively. And in section 9 he insisted that the competence of magistrates extends to both tables of the Decalogue, in other words, to the policing of man's relations with God as well as of those with his fellow man: upholding God's honour is their principal duty.

All this presupposed (a) a vigorous and independent Church, with a vigorous collegial clergy acting on its behalf; and (b) godly magistrates. Calvin's difficulty was that he needed a godly magistracy to second the 'spiritual' weapons employed by the clergy on recalcitrant congregations: although piety would have forbidden him to admit it, he never for a moment supposed that merely spiritual weapons would be enough; more palpable back-up from secular punishments and threats was indispensable to the 'building up' of the Church in the world. But a magistracy equipped with such power and legitimacy was well placed to interfere in the Church. What was needed, therefore, was a secular authority limited in its capacity to do evil, but not inhibited in any way in doing the work of God, with agencies to act as guarantors and sureties for its good behaviour. No such authority is attainable, for this would require the sanitization of power. Nevertheless, in so far as something could be done along these lines, Calvin did it.

It is possible to give for Calvin what it was impossible to give for Luther, a brief summary of his political theology. In the universe there is only one absolute and unconditionally authoritative *imperium, maiestas, puissance*: namely God's. All rightful authority in the world is directly or indirectly derived from God's. Unlike his followers and unlike the much more philosophically sophisticated Jesuit theologians and philosophers who opposed them and Divine Right alike, Calvin was not interested in the precise manner in which this derivative authority is attained; he speaks of it as being 'delegated', as 'legation' (the authority of a legate), as exercised by vice-gerents, 'representatives' (*vicarii, vices*), or *lieutenants* (place-holders or -takers). In connection with ecclesiastical authority, Calvin also speaks of 'envoys' or 'ambassadors'. But in each case his language recalls the metaphor of the relationship between an emperor and his subordinates, the point of the metaphor being of course to stress the extreme conditionality of the authority of the latter on the former. To denote the function of both civil and ecclesiastical governors, Calvin employs the words *ministerium, administratio, officium, functio* and *munus*, which incidentally echo fairly exactly Luther's terms *Dienst* and *Amt*. Such terms were highly congenial to Calvin, for duty is the key-note of his ethic. All authority in the world is an administering, doing the the work of someone else, under instruction. Calvin's preferred terms are *ministerium, administratio*; his very choice of words emphasizes that all authority in this world is conditional, limited and derivative. Conversely, he does on occasion use the term *imperium* interchangeably with *dominatio*, when his point is to stress the illegitimate extent of authority claimed by princes and popes; *dominatio* is here interchangeable with 'tyranny'. The function of such language is, of course, not in the least to minimize the significance of rightful authority. On the contrary, no more 'majestic' authority than one derived from God can be imagined. Rather, what is being said is that for as long as such authority confines itself to its proper 'office', it is invested with God's own majesty and dignity. But the moment magistrates exceed their measure of authority, they become (at least in respect of those particular actions, and perhaps wholly) akin to robbers, usurpers and invaders.

To designate a well-ordered polity, Calvin uses the term 'Christian polity', which arguably would have been a contradiction in terms for Luther. Since a Christian polity is characterized by a two-fold government, a double 'ministry' of magistrates and pastors, both deriving their authority from God, and both charged with governing the same body of persons, the only possible relationship between them is one of cooperation and mutual restraint, ideally complemented by some measure of restraint imposed on both in turn by the congregation/citizenry. The end at which this cooperation aims is the 'building up' (*aedificatio*, a Pauline term) of God's kingdom in the world.

'Restraint' is in some ways the notion best fitted to characterize Calvin's political theology and ecclesiology. Fallen humanity is constitutionally prone to wickedness, for which Calvin had a wide range of terms which modern English cannot match; the passions in each man are conceived by Calvin to resemble a boiling cauldron or a smouldering fire. Where there is no external restraint (as is notably the case with kings), the fire 'breaks out' and 'rages' (to use Calvin's and Luther's favourite terms for the conduct of the wicked and tyrants). The imposition of a 'bridle' or 'brake' is therefore indispensable. But restraining is not enough: for there is God's work to be done, and people must be *directed* to it. So that, whereas Luther's metaphor for the polity is the 'sword', Calvin's is the school or the 'bridle': the two-fold government imposes 'discipline', direction and restraint together.

A note on the translations

Texts used for these translations

For Luther's *Von Weltlicher Oberkeit* I have used the text in the Clemen edition.[1] I have also referred to the admirable East German students' edition, particularly valuable for its contextual information and footnotes,[2] and the modernized German version.[3] I have compared my translation, once completed, with that of J. J. Schindel.[4]

Luther never made the book accessible to a wider public by means of a Latin version, but he did not repudiate it either, for it was reprinted many times with his authority and he also refers to it in 1526 in his *Whether Soldiers too can be in a State of Grace*. An accurate and elegant Latin translation was made by Johann Lonitzer (Lonicerus) in 1525;[5] it tells us what an intelligent sixteenth-century Lutheran made of Luther, but has no independent authority. I have been unable to discover whether Luther was in any way directly associated with it; Lonitzer had formerly been his amanuensis. At any rate Latin editions of Luther's collected writings in the sixteenth century did not include it, whereas German collections always included *Von Weltlicher Oberkeit*. If Calvin

---

[1] O. Clemen (ed.), *Luthers Werke in Auswahl* (repr. Berlin: Walther de Gruyter and Co., 1967), vol. II, pp. 360–94.

[2] H. Erich Delius (ed.), *Studienausgabe* (Berlin: Evangelische Verlagsanstalt, 1982–), vol. III, pp. 27–71.

[3] K. von Ahland (ed.), *Luther Deutsch* (Göttingen: Vandenhoeck und Ruprecht, 1961–82).

[4] In J. Dillenberger (ed.), *Martin Luther Selections* (Garden City, NY: Anchor Books, 1961), and (in a revised version) in vol. XLV of *Luther's Works* (St Louis, Concordia, and Philadelphia: Fortress Press, 1966), pp. 75–130. This is a very competent translation.

[5] *De sublimiore mundi potestate, M. Lutheri Liber, donatus latinitate a Ioanne Lonicero*, no place of publication ((Strasbourg), 1525.). Lonitzer had been Luther's secretary, and was then teaching in Strasbourg.

was familiar with the work, it would have been in Lonitzer's translation. Another (partial) translation was made by Sebastien Châteillon (Castellio), and reprinted pseudonymously as a plea for toleration: *Martini Luteri* (some versions had *Aretii Cathari*) *de magistratu seculari, secunda pars*, in Martinus Bellius (pseud.), *De haereticis an sint persequendi . . . doctorum virum . . . sententiae*, Magdeburgi apud Georgium Rausch [pseud., in fact Basle,] 1554.

For Calvin's Latin *Institutio Christianae religionis* my text is that of P. Barth and W. Niesel,[6] collated with the French *Institution de la Religion Chrétienne* in the *Corpus Reformatorum*[7] edition. I have consulted the excellent edition and translation of J. T. McNeill and F. L. Battles[8] as well as the translation (done in 1561) by Thomas Norton, who worked (competently) with the 1559 Latin edition.[9] The much-reprinted Beveridge translation is mostly useless.

Aims of these translations

The brilliance of both Luther and Calvin as translators can only occasion despondency in lesser mortals attempting the same task. Their homogeneity of style and elegance of expression are quite beyond my capacity; all I have sought to provide is a text which does not constantly cause the reader to stumble, falter or pause, but which is entirely free of anachronism. I postulate readers who know that translation is ultimately impossible; who, although they cannot manage the originals, are prepared to acquire a familiarity with technical terms; and whose zeal will occasionally lead them to refer to the original. For such readers I have included in the Luther translation page references to the Clemen edition. Where my author uses the same term to clamp together a passage or perhaps the whole structure of his reflections (as for example Luther's *Oberkeit* and *weltlich*, or Calvin's *politia/police*), but relies on the range of connotation which their term has but no English term can match, I have not hesitated to include the original

[6] *Joannis Calvini Opera Selecta*, (Munich: C. Kaiser, 1926–36), vols. III – V.
[7] G. Baum, E. Cunitz and E. Reuss (eds.), *Joannis Calvini Opera quae supersunt Omnia, Corpus Reformatorum*, (Brunswick and Berlin: Berolini, 1863–1900), vol. IV.
[8] J. T. McNeill (ed.) and F. L. Battles (trans.), *Institutes of the Christian Religion*, Library of Christian Classics, (Philadelphia: Westminster Press, 1960), vols. XX and XXI.
[9] *The Institution of Christian Religion . . . according to the Author's Last Edition . . .* (London: Reinolde Wolfe and Richarde Harison, 1561). 'Last' means most recent (i.e. 1559); Calvin died in 1564.

term in brackets in the text, in modernized spelling in the case of Luther.

Stylistically, Luther's piece has proved particularly hard to handle, for there is no modern English genre which corresponds to it even approximately: although written and intended as a pamphlet, it reads like a sermon and is so described by Luther himself in the text. He could therefore afford to labour points to death (as it seems to us), be by turns folksy and erudite in the same paragraph, buttonhole his readers (hearers?), use free-floating demonstrative pronouns and adjectives ('this', 'that', 'it') without a second thought, and achieve precision by successive approximations of expression. A translation that reports all this faithfully, as the present one does, cannot fail to remind a reader that the original was not written by one of our contemporaries.

An approximate genre for Calvin's *Institution of the Christian Religion*, a treatise written in scholarly language, is admittedly not impossible to find, but it presents other difficulties which are just as intractable. There are two final versions: the Latin of 1559, and the French of 1560. The latter is so free a rendering that the editors of the *Corpus Reformatorum* and other scholars until well into this century held it to be the work of an amanuensis, and (according to some) not a very competent one at that. That view has now been decently buried, but the evidence adduced for it graphically underlines the discrepancies between the two versions. Both, however, are equally authentic and authoritative. Therefore, although I am offering a translation of the Latin version, I have kept the French in view in every line, signalling the more striking variations by means of a footnote (where a line or a whole passage is involved) or in the body of the text (where it is a matter of a word or two).

In the main, these discrepancies simply reflect the difference between sixteenth-century French and humanist Latin, and also the different audiences to which the two versions are addressed. The French version presupposed a less learned public and is therefore both more colloquial and in places more explicit. Presumably it was, for example, French colloquial usage which induced Calvin to refer systematically to 'Saint Peter' or 'Saint Paul' in the French versions, but simply to 'Paul' or 'Peter' in the Latin ones. Latin, on the other hand allowed Calvin to indulge his humanist passion for superlatives, emphatic words, pleonasms, copulatives, doublets, litotes, and for 'dignified' expression; he was reluctant to allow a verb to slip by without adorning it (as it seemed to him) with an adverb and seems to have thought nouns naked unless decently clad with some adjective; and no Old or New Testament figure ever 'says' anything: they 'declare', 'testify', 'bear witness'. In addition, an inflected language permits the almost limitless accumulation of dependent clauses and sub-clauses, especially when abetted by the use of the ablative absolute and the gerund. Sixteenth-century French was relatively tolerant of such things, just as it also viewed the free-floating demonstrative pronoun and adjective with equanimity, but it is closer to modern English in its structure and sensibility. And where Calvin himself ignored some copulative, pleonasm, emphatic word etc., or changed the structure of his sentences and paragraphs, or was indifferent about which precise word to use, when rendering his Latin into French, I have felt free to follow his example. I must admit that at times I have simply abandoned the unequal struggle to find an English-sounding equivalent for some humanist excrescence, and have simply taken the French. Conscience of course obliged me to signal the fact.

The 1559/1560 *Institutions* are the last of a long line of editions and translations which had begun in 1536. Calvin sometimes added entire new chapters and even recast the whole structure of the book, but more usually he used existing paragraphs from the previous version and interpolated additions, qualifications and amplifications. To allow readers to follow the movement of Calvin's opinions over the years, I have noted the dating of the most substantial interpolations. In the chapter translated here, the order of paragraphs remained unchanged.

Finally, both my authors fashioned their own translations from the Septuagint and the Hebrew for their copious citations from Scripture, but the old Church Vulgate was as much a part of the furniture of their minds as the Authorized Version (and for some of us, the Douay-Rheims-Challoner) is of ours. My translations are mostly taken from the AV, itself the product of men nurtured on the Genevan Bible, but depart from it where necessary. The practice of using modern Bible translations, as if this were what Luther or Calvin understood the Bible to say, is indefensible.

Chronology

at the Imperial Diet at Worms. Riots and iconoclasm at Wittenberg.

1522 **Luther**'s *Faithful Warning to all Christians to guard against riots and disturbances*. Publication of his German translation of the New Testament.

1523 **Luther** publishes *The Right and Power of a Christian Community to judge all doctrine and appoint and dismiss Teachers* and *On Secular Authority*.

1524–5 German Peasants' War. Müntzer preaches the coming end of the world.

1525 **Luther** publishes *Against the Heavenly Prophets*, *Admonition to Peace*, *Against the Robbing and Murdering Hordes of Peasants*, and *An Open Letter about the Harsh Book against the Peasants*. Marries Katharina von Bora. Zwingli publishes *On True and False Religion*. Erasmus' anti-Lutheran *On the Freedom of the Will*; **Luther** replies with *On the Enslaved Will*.

1526 **Luther** publishes *Whether Soldiers too can be in a State of Grace*.

1527 Quietist Anabaptists of Switzerland and Lower Germany publish the *Schleitheim Articles*.

1528 Imperial mandate threatens death penalty against Anabaptists

1529 Imperial Diet at Speyer, where Lutheran estates first given the name 'Protestants'.

1530 After failure of Emperor Charles V's attempts to reimpose Catholic orthodoxy at Imperial Diet of Augsburg, where Lutherans present their *Augsburg Confession*, Lutheran princes unite in the Schmalkaldic League against the Emperor and Catholic princes.

1531 Death of Zwingli in the battle of Kappel between Catholic and Protestant Swiss cantons. **Luther** publishes *Warning to his dear Germans*.

1532 **Calvin** publishes his *Commentary on Seneca's 'De Clementia'*.

1534 **Calvin** flees France for Basle after the Affair of the Placards and the subsequent persecution of French 'Lutherans'. First complete edition of **Luther**'s German Bible.

1534–5 Anabaptists take over Münster; their 'Kingdom' overthrown by joint Protestant–Catholic forces.

1535 Geneva declares reformation.

1536 First edition of **Calvin**'s *Institution of the Christian Religion*. **Calvin** appointed lecturer in Scripture at Geneva.

1537 **Calvin** writes the *Confession of Faith* and the *Catechism* for Geneva.

1538 **Calvin** expelled from Geneva; minister to the French congregation at Strasbourg.

1539 New, extended edition of the *Institution*. First volume of complete works of **Luther**.

1540 **Calvin** marries Idelette de Bure. Papacy formally establishes the Jesuit Order. **Calvin**'s *Reply to Cardinal Sadoleto's Letter to the Genevans* and his *Commentary on St Paul's Epistle to the Romans*.

1541 Failure of the Colloquy of Regensburg to reunite Catholics and Protestants. **Calvin** recalled to Geneva. First French version of **Calvin**'s *Institution*. Ecclesiastical Ordinances for Geneva implemented.

1542 **Calvin** publishes his *Psychopannychia*.

1543 Substantially revised edition of the *Institution* (Latin; French translation 1545).

1544 **Calvin**'s *Brief Admonition against the Anabaptists*.

1545 Council of Trent opens 13 December. **Luther** publishes his last anti-papal tract: *Against the Papacy at Rome, founded by the Devil*.

1546 **Luther** dies at Eisleben 18 February.

1547 Emperor defeats the Schmalkaldic League at Mühlberg and attempts to impose a religious compromise, the *Interim*. **Calvin**'s *Acts of the Council of Trent with The Antidote* and his *Adultero–German Interim*.

1548 **Calvin** publishes his *Commentaries on St Paul's Epistles to the Galatians, Ephesians, Philippians and Colossians*. French edition the same year.

1549 The *Zurich Consensus on the Matter of the Sacrament between Jean Calvin and the Church of Zurich*.

1551 **Calvin**'s collected *Commentaries on all the Epistles of St Paul*.

1553 Servetus executed at Geneva for heresy. Theodore de Bèze (**Calvin's** collaborator and later successor) publishes *The Punishment of Heretics by the Civil Magistrate*.

1554 Sebastien Châteillon (Castellio) publishes *Whether Heretics are to be Persecuted*.

1555 Peace of Augsburg stabilizes existing territorial divisions between Catholic and Protestant states in the Empire. Charles V abdicates.

1556   French edition of all of **Calvin**'s *Commentaries* on all the New Testament Epistles.

1558   Death of Charles V. John Knox publishes *First Blast of the Trumpet against the Monstrous Regiment of Women*.

1559   Last Latin edition of **Calvin**'s *Institution*. Establishment of the Genevan Academy with Theodore de Bèze as its first Rector. Henri II of France dies, succeeded by François II and (in 1560) Charles IX, both minors, with Catherine de' Medici as Regent and the fiercely anti-Protestant Guise family dominant at court.

1560   Huguenot Conspiracy of Amboise. First Edict of Toleration for French Huguenots. Publication of the Genevan Bible in English. Last French edition of **Calvin**'s *Institution*.

1561   The Colloquy of Poissy fails to restore unity between Huguenots and Catholics. Thomas Norton's translation of **Calvin**'s *Institution of Christian Religion*.

1562   *Confession of Faith of the Reformed Churches of France*. Massacre of Huguenots at Vassy by the Duke of Guise. First French War of Religion.

1563   Peace of Amboise gives Huguenot communities a degree of toleration. Council of Trent closes with publication of Decrees.

1564   **Calvin** dies at Geneva on 27 May.

Glossary

Luther

Authority, those in authority, rulers, superiority, superiors:
Oberkeit, *Oberen*; see also **Power**

The word rendered throughout this translation as 'authority', 'those in authority' or 'the authorities' is *Oberkeit*, an abstract term meaning either the status of having authority or power (*q.v.*), or the collectivity of those enjoying such a status. Luther moved readily from the abstract *Oberkeit* to the personal *die Oberen* ('superiors'), signifying persons of superior political status. This translation of *Oberkeit* as 'authority' is far from felicitous. It not only implies a distinction between 'authority' and 'power' which Luther precisely did *not* make. It also suggests an abstract quality to Luther's thought which it lacks: when speaking of *Oberkeit* he thought in terms of persons (and more often than not one person, a prince [*Fürst*] or lord [*Herr*]), equipped with power (see Introduction, p. xiv). He alternated freely between 'authority' (*Oberkeit*) and 'those in authority' (*die Oberen*). Sometimes, in order to preserve this verbal link or to signal the personalizing character of the thought, I have had to resort to the now obsolete terms 'superiority' (instead of 'authority') and 'superiors' (e.g. pp. 33, 39) to translate *Oberkeit*.

Luther himself used the Saxon dialect *Uberkeit* (in various spellings, and in one version *Oberkeytt*), which was rendered in contemporary High German as *Oberkeit*. This term was later replaced by *Obrigkeit*, which has in turn become obsolete, except as a deliberate archaism (like the English expressions 'the powers that be', or 'our lords and masters').

Degree, see **estate**
Duty, see **office**
Earth, earthly, see **world**

Estate, state, station, status, standing, rank, condition, degree: *Stand*; see also **office, superiors**

Stand is a collective term for all those sharing the same legal or social status or rank, and is precisely comparable in meaning to the English terms of the time 'degree' ('a person of low degree') or 'estate' (as in 'estates of the realm', the French Estates General; the German equivalent is the *Reichstände* [Imperial Diet] of the Holy Roman Empire). The most significant theological use Luther made of this term was to deny the traditional distinction between those with a (superior) 'spiritual' or ecclesiastical status, and those of an (inferior) lay status, and indeed to counter the tendency to equate spiritual and ecclesiastical status. The theologically salient distinction amongst humans, in Luther's view, is between the Christian and the Unchristian; amongst the former, there are only differences of 'office' (*q.v.*) or function. All Christians are in this sense members of the same 'Christian estate', i.e., the collectivity of those enjoying the status of Christians. All of them have 'Christian liberty' and all are equally priests, as far as their spiritual status is concerned (e.g. p. 8). This, however, according to Luther's doctrine, leaves secular distinctions of rank untouched, and does not abolish the need for a differentiation of 'offices' or 'tasks' (*q.v.*).

However, Luther also used the term *Stand* in the sense which was more conventional at the time, to refer to the idea of a hierarchical order in civil society, within which each individual has a certain rank or place. Thus there are superiors and inferiors, and among superiors there are higher (emperors, kings and princes) and lower (lords; cf. e.g. p. 39 and fn. 54) and equally, there are different occupations or ways of life. In this sense, the term 'estate' is sometimes interchangeable with 'office', 'occupation' or 'job'; e.g. p. 7 and fn 12; the soldiering *Stand*; pp. 35, 36: the prince's *Stand*; pp. 18–19: the *Stand oder Amt* of a cobbler, preacher or married person (the 'married state'); in the same paragraph (students of Max Weber may care to note) Luther uses the term 'vocation' or 'calling' (*Beruffung*) synonymously with both *Stand* and *Amt*.

Force, see **power**
Function, see **office**
Government, see **kingdom**

Just: *Fromm*; see also **law**; and cf. Glossary: Calvin – **dutiful**

Luther frequently used the word *fromm* where modern German would use *gerecht*, although he also used the latter term; in Luther's time, *fromm* was still equivalent to the Latin terms *iustus, probus, bonus*; it seems also to serve him for *pius* (one of the meanings which the Brothers Grimm's *Deutsches Wörterbuch* gives for *fromm*, although it lists no instance of Luther using the terms equivalently, p. 241), which meant 'dutiful' (cf. Glossary: Calvin – dutifulness) and hence 'just', in the sense of doing the duties one owes, whether these be to God, or to men, or both. In *On Secular Authority* Luther frequently did not distinguish, when using this term, between the merely outwardly just (i.e. those who conform to rules and laws) and the inwardly or truly just. Thus on both p. 6 and p. 7, rulers are said to have the duty to punish the 'wicked' and protect the *Frommen*. The English equivalent terms in the sixteenth century were 'godly' and 'righteous', the latter being perhaps the more apt, but since they too are unintelligible to a modern reader, I have felt unable to use them here, although there are points in the Calvin translation where I found them irresistible. I have translated *fromm* throughout as 'just'. Cf. especially p. 10 fn. 15 and the Introduction, p. xiii.

Law, right: *Recht, Gesetz*; see also **just**

The German term *Recht*, like the French *droit*, Italian *diritto*, Spanish *derecho*, and Latin *ius*, has always been a translator's nightmare. Its meaning encompasses any, or any combination, of the following: what is right or just; justice; a right (i.e. an entitlement, whether legal or moral); the law (as an academic discipline, or in the sense of 'the law of the land', the corpus of laws of a polity). It is thus more general in reference than the English word 'law' which I have generally been obliged to use in order to render it. It can also form an adjective or an adverb (and, in an obsolete form still used in Luther's time, a verb: *rechten*, 'to go to court'; cf. modern German *richten*, 'to judge', but also 'to mend' or 'repair'; and *berechtigt*, 'entitled', 'justified in'). Luther, like his contemporaries, was by and large disinclined to stress the distinction, which is obscured by the term *Recht*, between what is legally and what is morally right, or between having a legal and having a moral right. He took it that the law of the land usually merely codifies or enforces the moral law (a precisely similar view of law is implicit in Calvin's *Institution*, section 16), and therefore that the true Christian is naturally law-abiding, indeed that the true Christian does not need the positive law at all. Cf. his arguments on pp. 9–11.

His term for 'just persons' is sometimes *die Gerechten*, but more usually *die Frommen*. His term for justice is *Recht* (cf. *above*) or *Gerechtigkeit*, and for 'wrong' or 'a wrong' or 'injustice' it is *Unrecht*.

Luther also used the term *Gesetz* (from *setzen* or *satzen*, to 'lay down' or 'set down'), which means 'positive', 'made', or 'statute' law (like Calvin's term *constitutio*, see Calvin fn. 71). Quite often he paired *Recht* and *Gesetz* (e.g. p. 7), or attached no significance to the distinction. But *Gesetz* clearly implies a law-maker (like the Roman *lex*), and means a specific law, whereas *Recht* means law in general and does not necessarily imply any reference to any law-maker. Luther thought of law as contained in books (e.g. p. 34). He thought law-codices were bound to generate commentaries (of the scholastic sort which he deplored), which would be regarded as authoritative for the interpretation of the laws, and these he also described as 'books' (cf. Introduction, pp. xiii–xiv).

Kingdom, kingship, governments: *Reich*, *Regiment*; see also **authority, secular**

The term translated here as 'kingdom' or 'kingship' is *Reich*. Luther's term *Regiment* is always translated in this version as 'government'. Thus a *Reich* has, or entails, a *Regiment*, and a *Regiment* governs a *Reich*. In *On Secular Authority*, Luther adhered to this distinction consistently. However, he also used the term *die Gewalt* interchangeably with *Regiment*, and '(secular) authority' ([*weltliche*] *Oberkeit*) interchangeably with both, and thus I have not infrequently been obliged to use the term 'government' for all of these terms (see power, authority).

Luther's term *Reich* mimics fairly closely the range of referents of the classical and medieval term *imperium* (cf. Glossary: Calvin – authority), which has the modern connotations of the term 'empire' as well as its obsolete ones (as, for example, in the expressions 'the empire of opinion', or 'the empire of the law'); in other words it means 'ruling', and 'what is ruled over'. In the former sense, it approximates to the term 'sovereignty', or at least supreme authority. In medieval and early modern Latin both emperors and kings (but not lesser rulers and princelings) are said to have *imperium*, and precisely the same applies to *Reich*. The term does not distinguish between 'kingship' and 'kingdom', or 'principate' and 'principality'.

God's *Reich*, as Luther understands it, means two things: first, his governance and sovereignty over the whole universe, in which sense both the elect and the reprobate, and indeed Satan himself, are subject to God's 'empire'; and second: God's kingship over his chosen people, the elect, in other words, the invisible universal Church of the Saints, living, dead and as yet unborn (e.g. p. 6). Confusingly, God's *Reich* has two 'governments' (*Regimente*), the 'spiritual' and the 'secular' (*q.v.*), and it is not clear whether Luther means that the 'spiritual' *Regiment* corresponds to God's governance over the elect only, whereas the 'secular' or 'temporal' or 'earthly' *Regiment* is God's government over the reprobate *and* the elect, or only over the reprobate. The latter seems to be Luther's meaning on p. 10, where he speaks of the 'kingdom (*Reich*) of the world', and of the 'secular government' (*Regiment*) as having been established 'outside the Christian estate'. At any rate, the symbol and characteristic implement of the secular *Regiment* is the Sword, and on various occasions Luther speaks of the 'Government of (or by) the Sword' (see Introduction). If it was indeed Luther's view that secular government is exclusively over the unrighteous, then the Christian's relationship to secular government is not true subjection at all, but merely an implicate of his duty to participate in God's *Reich* in the first sense. But at various points even in this work, a more positive interpretation of the function of secular *Regiment* shows through: it is sometimes construed as a 'help' to our weaker neighbours in need, who may (in the end) prove to be 'elect' after all; the 'judgement of charity' demands that we assume people to be potentially elect. Sometimes (e.g. p. 33) Luther appears to use 'spiritual *Regiment*' merely to mean the government of bishops and priests over *visible* churches (the terms he was using at this time, when he cared to make any distinction at all, were 'bodily' or 'external' churches), which contain both the elect and the unrighteous, but then proceeds to explain that those who are not true Christians belong to the *Reich* of the world, and are subject to external *Regiment*. The terminology of the two *Reiche* therefore shares the ambiguities of Luther's vocabulary of world/secular/temporal (*q.v.* and cf. Introduction, pp. xi–xiii).

Regiment is an abstract term, but Luther tends to think of it as a person or body of persons who rule(s), or the collectivity of those subject to such rulers (see authority, *above*); e.g. pp. 11, 12 where Luther speaks, counterfactually, of a 'Christian *Regiment*', i.e. a collectivity composed of governors and governed who are all true Christians. There is no significant difference in the level of abstractness of thought whether Luther is using *Regiment*, *Oberkeit* or *die Oberen*, or indeed *die Gewalt* (see power)

Office, occupation, vocation or **calling, duty, service, task**: *Amt, Beruffung, Dienst*; see also **estate** and cf. Glossary: Calvin – **dutifulness**

The vocabulary Luther uses to designate tasks, duties, occupations and service is very unspecific. *Amt* denotes an 'occupation', 'profession', 'job' and the duties and responsibilities that go with it; sometimes it denotes someone's 'work' – and indeed Luther often uses the term *Werk* – or 'task' (e.g. the *Amt* of Christ or St John the Baptist; in other words what they came into the world to do; Luther even speaks of the *Amt* of the law). Luther uses *Amt* interchangeably with *Beruffung* (vocation) and *Stand* (see estate). The German word seems to parallel the Latin *officium* (cf. Glossary: Calvin – office), meaning a 'duty' or 'duties' attendant on a status, as well as a 'position', 'occupation' or 'office' (e.g. a government office). One's duty may of course be a service to others, and *Dienst* (service) is often used interchangeably with 'office' or 'duty'.

Power, violence, force: *Gewalt*; see also **authority**

Luther's use of the term *Gewalt* is treated in the Introduction, pp. xv–xvi. The comments on Calvin's use of *potestas* and *imperium* are also relevant (see Glossary: Calvin – authority). The crucial point is that *Gewalt* erodes the distinction between 'power' and 'authority'. This is hardly surprising, given Luther's 1523 view of the proper function of government as repressive and punitive; repressing and punishing can be done as well by those whose power is illegitimate as by those with legitimate power. Sometimes (e.g. pp. 29, 30, 33) Luther uses *Gewalt* in the sense of mere 'force' or 'violence'; sometimes neutrally, like the English word 'power', (e.g. pp. 14, 28); and often as a synonym for 'authority', 'those in power', or 'the authorities', 'government', 'superiority' (*q.v.*), e.g. pp. 6, 14, 20, 21, 25.

Rank, see **estate**
Right, see **law**

Secular, temporal, worldly: *Weltlich*

The difficulties connected with translating *weltlich* are discussed in the Introduction, p. xii. In one sense, the world (*Welt*) is simply 'this life' and everything connected with it and therefore includes Christians and Unchristians alike; in another sense it is 'the worldly', as opposed to 'true Christians', the 'earth' as contrasted to 'heaven'. In the same way, the adjective *weltlich* sometimes refers neutrally to things, whether good or bad, related to this world, but it can also carry the pejorative meaning of 'worldliness', or falling short of spiritual standards. In the former sense, the appropriate translation is 'secular' or 'temporal'; in the latter, it has to be rendered as 'worldly'. In some places (pp. 27 and 32) Luther is deliberately playing on the ambiguity of the German term; in other places (e.g. pp. 10–11) it may be that the negative connotations of the term have proved inimical to clarity of thought, especially given the generally hostile attitude towards 'secular' rulers that Luther takes in this text.

Service, see **office**
State, see **estate**
Standing, see **estate**
Station, status, see **estate**
Superiority, superiors, see **authority, power**
Sword, see **authority**, and Introduction, p. xvi
Task, see **office**
Temporal, see **secular**
Violence, see **power**
World, worldly, see **secular**

Calvin

Authority, power: *potestas, autoritas* (*sic*), *imperium, dominatio; puissance, authorité, domination*

'Authority' and 'power' in this translation render a variety of Latin and

French terms in Calvin's texts. I see no evidence that he was using these terms to make any distinctions; he seems simply to have been adhering to the stylistic norm that one should seek variety, rather than repeating the same term in the same sentence or consecutive sentences. He therefore unwittingly followed scholastic rather than classical usage; the latter certainly would not have used *auctoritas* and *potestas* interchangeably (nor spelt the former *autoritas*, as Calvin does). At any rate, *potestas* in this text means the 'powers', rights or entitlements to do, that go with a particular office; or simply 'authority' in the abstract. *Imperium* in classical Latin is the complex of powers that inhere in the highest civic offices, notably those of a consul, praetor or general, later those of an emperor; in medieval and early modern Latin, the term's use was extended to include the rights of the kingly office. Thus *imperium* is the highest *potestas*, in so far as there is any distinction. *Auctoritas* in classical Latin meant personal or moral authority, the right to a respectful hearing which is acquired by experience, success and respectable status; but Calvin uses the term, as scholastic writers did, as a synonym for *imperium* or *potestas* (e.g. ss. 23, 25). He also of course uses it (and *authorité*) when he means moral or intellectual authority.

All three terms connote legitimacy in Calvin's usage, and this fact has governed my translation, but it also creates difficulties. The English term 'power' is quite neutral as to legitimacy, although it is frequently used interchangeably with 'authority'; the latter term however always denotes a right to act, whereas 'power' may mean no more than a capacity to achieve intended effects, the control of resources to induce others to do what they would not otherwise do, and may thus have nothing to do with 'authority'; the latter in turn may exist without 'power'. Since Calvin is concerned throughout to stress the entitlement of the 'powers that be' to obedience, and was not prepared to indulge speculations about legitimacy or the lack of it, I have consistently rendered *autoritas*, *potestas* and *imperium* as 'authority', except in those passages where 'power' is established in English (as for example in the translation of the critical passage in Romans 13 (ss. 4 and 23); or where the emphasis is indeed on 'power' (as for example s. 10); in these cases I have given the original term in brackets. It has not seemed worth while to signal whether the original has *imperium* or *potestas*, since Calvin used them interchangeably in the same line or successive lines (e.g. s. 24). In one place Calvin does distinguish 'power' from 'authority' by using the Latin term *potentia* ('might'), which carries no suggestion of legitimacy. The French version translates all three terms indifferently as *puissance*, as may be seen in the appended translation of s. 8, where I have given the original terms, although it usually (for no discernible reason apart from the immediacy of the suggestion) renders *autoritas* as *authorité*. In one place it even renders *ius* ('right') as *puissance*. Even more strangely, Calvin uses *dominatio/domination* as an equivalent for all the other terms, although in republican times, this (because it relates to the rule of a *dominus* over subjects or slaves) would have been deemed to confuse household and civil relations. Calvin had no scruples on this score either in French or Latin, although he uses *dominatio* when he speaks of the power of tyrants (e.g. s. 30).

Although arguments from silence are tricky, I cannot forbear to note that the term 'sovereign' occurs, I think, only once in the French text, in the expression *l'empire souverain*, where the reference is to God's power, as contrasted with earthly power (*puissance terrienne*); the Latin text here merely refers to God's *ius*; and Calvin gets no closer to any term for 'sovereignty' than *imperium*. 'Sovereignty' is of course recognizably not a term with a classical Latin pedigree; Latin versions of it would be *plenitudo potestatis*, or *plena* (or *summa*) *potestas* (or *autoritas*); the latter term appears in the text in s. 31, where Calvin is emphasizing the duty of obedience of private persons, but is immediately followed by the reference to the rights of 'popular magistrates'. An alternative way of rendering 'sovereignty' in Latin, *merum imperium*, appears in s. 32; the reference here is to God's power.

The term *maiestas* is freely used by Calvin for both divine and secular authority; it too was a possible Latin synonym for 'sovereignty'. As Calvin uses it, however, it is not a legal term; from classical times it had had a religious aura, and it was this aspect of it that Calvin found serviceable.

Civil order, see **polity**
Commonwealth, see **polity**

Dutifulness, duty, service to God, piety, impiety, godliness, righteousness: *pietas*, *pieté*

The two sixteenth- and seventeenth-century English terms that adequately rendered *pietas* (*pieté*) are 'righteousness' and (more accurately still) 'godliness'. On some occasions no other terms will do. For the most part, despite their clumsiness, I have resorted to the periphrases 'dutifulness' or 'service to God'. 'Pious' (which some translators use, no doubt to cut their losses and in desperation) is hopelessly inappropriate; a 'pious prince' in modern English would be one constantly at his devotions, and students of Latin will remember 'pius Aeneas'. (The opposite 'impious', being entirely obsolete, is unobjectionable but also does little service to the reader.)

Calvin used *pius*, which is precisely equivalent to Luther's *fromm* (see Glossary: Luther – just) in its strict classical sense, i.e. ready to do one's duty, whether it be to God, to men, to ancestors, or to religion; he sometimes pairs *pietas* with *iustitia* ('justice'), so that the pair means duties to God and to men; perfect justice (or 'righteousness') would be perfection in dutifulness to both God and men, justice being to give everyone their due.

Form of government, see **polity**
Godliness, see **dutifulness**

Magistrate, prince: *magistratus, princeps/ magistrat, prince*; see also *superiors*

Calvin habitually uses the republican word *magistratus* ('magistrate') as the generic term for an 'officeholder' (see esp. ss. 3–4); it is interchangeable with 'superior' (*praefectus, supérieur q.v.*), but more definitely intimates an elective manner of appointment; the electors need not of course be the whole citizenry. Calvin's point was not so much to stress the subordination of officeholders to electors, but rather their subordination to God. This is also the point of his repeated description of magistrates as 'ministers' (i.e. servants, e.g. in s. 7.), 'representatives', 'legates', 'lieutenants' etc. His contemporaries, Luther included, would for the most part have employed the expression 'kings and princes' and would have used 'magistrates' to designate the holders of inferior offices, especially judicial ones, or the elective rulers of cities. Nevertheless, it should be noted that Calvin himself often uses *prince* or *supérieur* in the French version to translate *magistratus* (e.g. ss. 17, 22, 23, 31, 32).

Piety, see **dutifulness**
Prince, see **magistrate**

Polity, civil order, regime, form of government, commonwealth:
politia, ordinatio, regimen, gubernatio, respublica, civitas; police, ordonnance, chose publique, république

Calvin, like his French- and German-speaking contemporaries, had no word exactly equivalent to the modern term 'state' (and those translations which do use the term to render some word of Calvin's invariably mean no more than 'government'). But he did use a range of Latin abstract terms and their French derivatives for which Luther, and German-speakers generally until the very end of the sixteenth century and beyond, had no equivalent; the only German term available to Luther himself was *Gemeinde*. Given his republican leanings, Calvin needed a more abstract term than Luther, who mostly designated the civil association by reference to the form of government (as 'kingdom', 'principality', 'duchy', 'electorate', 'empire' etc.), and I have generally rendered Calvin's terms as 'polity', or by its sixteenth-century equivalent, 'commonwealth'. Once again, as far as I can discern, Calvin did not use these various terms to make distinctions, but simply for the sake of elegance, *copia verborum*; indeed he often uses *regimen* or *gubernatio* ('government') when he might equally well have spoken of *politia*, and vice versa (e.g. s. 8, Latin version); however, he also used the latter term in a technical sense which is discussed in fn. 31.

Of this group of synonyms, the word most difficult to render satisfactorily is (*publica*) *ordinatio, ordonnance*. Not indeed that it says anything difficult to understand; the difficulty is rather that of echoing the overtones of the original. The only approximation is the word 'order', which I have used *faute de mieux*. It means 'that which orders', 'that which has been put in order', where 'order' may mean either 'command' or 'good order' or both. Usually *ordinatio* just means 'the public order' or 'government' (e.g. ss. 1 and 2, where it is merely a variant for *regimen*, and s. 3, where it is an alternative for *politia/police*). *Politia* in turn is 'the civil order', and is interchangeable (e.g. in ss. 8, 9 and 14) with *respublica, civitas, chose publique, république*. It is not clear whether Calvin had ever read Claude de Seyssel's *La Monarchie de France* (1516), in which Seyssel uses *la police* to mean the institutional order or (although this rendering is in important respects anachronistic) the 'constitution'; at any rate, he sometimes means by *politia* the institutional order, an order of laws and institutions which make up a civil association. 'Laws' and its various European cognates, until at least the eighteenth century, meant not only 'rules', but also the institutions and arrangements constituted and framed by those rules. This is also at least part of the meaning of the expression he uses three times in this chapter (ss. 3 and 14): *politia Christiana* ('Christian polity'), and when he speaks of the *politia* of the Jews (ss. 15 and 16).

Power, see **authority**
Regime, see **polity**
Righteousness, see **dutifulness**
Rulers, see **superiors**

Service to God, see **dutifulness**
Superiors, superiority, rulers, government, (pre)eminence: *praefectus, praefectura, supérieurs, supériorité*; see also **magistrate, office**

Calvin did not personalize political authority nearly as much as Luther did. He stressed the distinction between office and occupant much more, and he never assumed that every office of authority was to be construed as being on one rung of a ladder or gradation, on which each individual up to the emperor has a superior. Nevertheless, he too was heavily reliant on the notion of the polity as composed of relations of command and obedience, superior and subject. He too, therefore, used terms which closely match Luther's *Oberkeit* and *Oberen*, namely *praefectura* and *praefecti* (and even more closely: *supérieur* and *supériorité*); *praefectura* is often enough (e.g. s. 4) merely a synonym for 'government'. The Latin terms (though not the French), however, intimate an 'appointment', 'designation', 'installation' (from *praeficere*; to place or set someone before, or in charge of, someone else); my translation, like Calvin's French, loses this connotation. Since we no longer talk of 'superiors' and 'inferiors' in this context, my translation must be archaic if it is to reflect Calvin's thought.

Calvin also uses other metaphors of height or elevation to symbolize status, such as 'eminence'.

Notes on further reading

Luther

For an introductory overview of the Reformation, G. R. Elton, *Reformation Europe, 1517–1555* (London: Fontana, 1963) is very serviceable. S. E. Ozment, *The Reformation in the Cities* (New Haven and London: Yale University Press, 1975) exemplifies well one of the approaches more recent Reformation studies are taking.

The most accessible biography of Luther is that of James Atkinson, *Martin Luther and the Birth of Protestantism* (London: Marshall Morgan and Scott, rev. edn. 1982); but see also A. G. Dickens, *Martin Luther and the Reformation* (London: Hodder, 1967). For a general survey of Luther's political thought, the best book in English is W. D. J. Cargill Thompson, *The Political Thought of Martin Luther* (Sussex: Harvester, 1984), edited from an incomplete (and alas unfootnoted) manuscript by P. Broadhead after the author's death. Cargill Thompson took some account of the outstanding German work on Luther, notably that of Johannes Heckel, which still remains untranslated. Two articles by Thompson also repay study: 'Luther and the Right of Resistance to the Emperor', *Studies in Church History*, 12 (1975), and 'The "Two Kingdoms" and the "Two Regiments": Some Problems of Luther's *Zwei-Reiche-Lehre*', *Journal of Theological Studies*, 20 (1969), reprinted in Cargill Thompson, *Studies in the Reformation: Luther to Hooker* (London: Athlone Press, 1980). F. E. Cranz, *An Essay on the Development of Luther's Thought on Justice, Law and Society* (Cambridge, Mass.: Harvard University Press, 1959), and E. G. Rupp, 'Luther and Government', in H. Königsberger (ed.), *Luther* (London: Macmillan, 1973) are also well worth consulting. Rupp's *The Righteousness of God* (London: Hodder, 1953) will still serve very well as an introduction to

Luther's theology. B. A. Gerrish, 'John Calvin on Luther', in J. Pelikan (ed.), *Interpreters of Luther* (Philadelphia: Fortress Press, 1968), considers the relationship between the two theologians. The general topic of Church and polity in Reformation thought is discussed by J. M. Tonkin, *The Church and the Secular Order in Reformation Thought* (New York and London: Columbia University Press, 1971). The interpretative essay on Luther in S. S. Wolin, *Politics and Vision* (London: George Allen and Unwin, 1961), ch. 5, is also still worth considering for its magisterial sweep and seductive oversimplifications. And, of course, no bibliography on Luther could pretend to adequacy even at an introductory level unless it referred readers to Q. Skinner, *The Foundations of Modern Political Thought*, vol. II (Cambridge: Cambridge University Press, 1978).

For further study of Luther's thought, the most complete and accessible one-volume collection of unabridged (but not surprisingly, given how much it includes, mostly unfootnoted) translations is J. Dillenberger (ed.), *Martin Luther: Selections from his Writings* (New York: Doubleday, 1961). Those who intend to delve more deeply into Luther's 'political' writings will wish to consult the translations in *Luther's Works* (Philadelphia: Fortress Press, 1962–71) for the following tracts (the volumes in this edition in which they may be found are given in brackets):

The Freedom of a Christian, 1520 (31)
Address to the Christian Nobility of the German Nation, 1520 (44)
On Good Works, 1520 (44)
On the Papacy at Rome, 1520 (39)
A sincere Admonition by Martin Luther to all Christians to guard against Insurrection and Rebellion, 1522 (45)
That a Christian Assembly or Congregation has the Right and Power to judge all Teaching and to call, appoint and dismiss Teachers, 1523 (39)
On Trade and Usury, 1524 (45)
To the Councillors of all Cities in Germany, that they should Establish and Maintain Christian Schools, 1524 (45)
An Admonition to Peace, 1525 (46)
Against the Robbing and Murdering Hordes of Peasants, 1525 (46)
An Open Letter about the Harsh Book against the Peasants, 1525 (46)
Whether Soldiers too can be saved, 1526 (46)
Warning to his Dear German People, 1531 (47)

Calvin

Those entirely new to the topic can do much worse than to make a start with M. Mullett, *Calvin* (London: Routledge, 1989). The best biographies of Calvin are T. H. L. Parker, *John Calvin: A Biography* (Philadelphia: Westminster University Press, 1977) and W. J. Bouwsma, *John Calvin: A Sixteenth Century Portrait* (Oxford: Oxford University Press, 1988). To these should now be added A. E. McGrath, *A Life of John Calvin* (Oxford: Blackwell, 1990). As a synoptic account of Calvin's theology, F. Wendel, *Calvin: The Origins and Development of his Religious Thought* (London: Collins, 1963) is still indispensable. The current state of Calvin studies is surveyed and exemplified in R. V. Schnucker (ed.), *Calviniana: The Ideas and Influence of Jean Calvin*, in *Sixteenth Century Essays and Studies*, vol. X (Kirksville: Sixteenth Century Journal Publishers Inc., 1988). There is an excellent article on Geneva's foreign policy by R. Oresko: 'The Question of the Sovereignty of Geneva after the Treaty of Cateau-Cambrésis', in H. Königsberger (ed.), *Republiken und Republikanismus im Europa der Frühen Neuzeit* (Munich: Oldenbourg Verlag, 1988).

On Calvin's political thought, S. S. Wolin, *Politics and Vision* (London: George Allen and Unwin, 1961), ch. 6, is admirable. For a fuller discussion, the reader is referred to H. M. Höpfl, *The Christian Polity of John Calvin* (Cambridge: Cambridge University Press, 1982), and its bibliography. The best survey of the political thought of Calvin's disciples is Q. Skinner, *The Foundations of Modern Political Thought* (Cambridge: Cambridge University Press, 1978).

For further study of Calvin's writings, the best one-volume collection is J. Dillenberger, *John Calvin: Selections from his Writings* (Garden City, New York: Doubleday and Company, 1971), which includes the *Draft Ecclesiastical Ordinances* of 1541 and selections from other works. But for more detailed study of Calvin's *Institution of the Christian Religion*, the two-volume translation and edition, with copious introduction and footnotes by F. L. Battles (trans.) and J. T. McNeill (ed.), *Institutes of the Christian Religion*, (Philadelphia: Library of Christian Classics, 1960), vols. XX and XXI is the only complete translation which meets modern scholarly standards. As the introduction to the present work makes clear, a satisfactory understanding of Calvin's political thought demands attention to his ecclesiastical thought; Bk IV, chs. 1–12 are the crucial chapters here.

On Secular Authority

Luther: On Secular Authority: how far does the Obedience owed to it extend?
[*Von Weltlicher Oberkeit*]

Translator's note

Square brackets indicate words needed to complete the sense in the translation which are not in the original text. They are also used in Luther's scriptural references where, as not infrequently, they are inaccurate or Luther did not supply them, and to give verse references. Neither Luther nor his contemporaries cited the latter.

Words followed by an asterisk are explained and discussed in the Glossary.

Numbers in square brackets (e.g. [369:]) are page references to the Clemen edition of *Luthers Werke*.

[360:] To the illustrious and noble Prince and Lord, John, Duke of Saxony, Landgrave of Thüringen and Margrave of Meissen, my gracious Lord

Grace and peace in Christ. The force of circumstances, and the fact that many have asked me, but above all your Grace's [express] wishes, my most excellent and noble Prince and gracious Lord, oblige me to write once again about secular authority and its Sword: how can a Christian use be made of it and how far do Christians owe it obedience? What disturbs those [who have asked me to write] is Christ's words in Matthew 5 [25,39–40]: 'resist not evil . . . but be compliant with your opponent, and the person who takes your coat, let him also take your cloak.' And Romans 12 [19]: 'Vengeance is mine, says the Lord, I will repay.' It is precisely these texts that Prince Volusian long ago used in objection to [361:] St Augustine, impugning Christian doctrine for

3

giving evil-doers a free hand, and for being incompatible with the secular Sword.

The sophists at the universities have also found a stumbling-block here, since they could not square the two [the Sword and Christ's words]. So, in order not to put princes outside Christianity altogether,[1] they have taught that these sayings of Christ are not commands, but merely 'counsels of perfection'. In other words, to save the standing and dignity of princes, Christ had to be made out to be saying what was neither true nor right. They could not exalt princes without abasing Christ, blind wretched sophists that they are. This poisonous error has now pervaded the whole world and the common opinion about these sayings of Christ is that they are merely advice for those who want to be perfect, rather than binding commands intended for each and every Christian. [The sophists] have gone so far as to allow the [use of the] Sword and secular authority to the 'perfect' estate* of bishops, and even to the 'most perfect' estate of all, that of the pope. In fact, they have not merely allowed them [to make use of what properly belongs only to][2] this 'imperfect' estate of the Sword and secular authority; on the contrary, they have made them over wholly to the pope, more than to anyone else on earth. The devil has taken complete possession of the sophists and the universities; even they themselves no longer realize what they are saying and teaching.

But my hope is that I may be able to teach princes and secular authorities how they can remain Christians and yet leave Christ as Lord, without reducing Christ's commands to mere 'counsels' for their sake. And I wish to accomplish [this task] as a humble service to Your Grace, as something for all to make use of if they need it, and to the praise and glory of Christ our Lord. And I commend Your Grace and all your kin to God's grace, to keep them in his mercy. Amen.

Wittenberg, New Year's Day, 1523
Your Grace's humble servant
Martinus Luther

---

[1] Literally: to make princes into pagans. Scholastic theologians (the 'sophists') standardly reconciled the hard sayings of Christ to which Luther refers with the exigencies of practice by distinguishing between what was necessary for 'perfection' and what was adequate for those less spiritually ambitious.

[2] Luther's casual habits of expression and the obsolete conceptual equipment of 'estates' (for which see the Glossary) here makes an expansion necessary.

4

Some time ago, I wrote a pamphlet to the German nobility.[3] In it I set out their tasks and duties as Christians. How much notice they took of it is plain for all to see. And so I must turn my efforts in another direction and write instead about what they ought *not* to do, and *desist* from doing. I am confident that they will pay as little attention this time as they did to my last piece. Long may they remain princes, and never become Christians. [362:] For God Almighty has driven our princes mad: they really think they can command their subjects whatever they like and do with them as they please. And their subjects are just as deluded, and believe (wrongly) that they must obey them in all things. It has now come to this, that rulers have begun to order people to hand over books[4] and to believe and think as their rulers tell them. They have had the temerity to put themselves in God's place, to make themselves masters of consciences and belief[5] and to undertake to give lessons to the Holy Spirit from what is in their addled brains. And after all that, they will not allow anyone to dare to tell them [the truth], and still insist on being called 'My gracious Lords'.

They write and issue edicts, [pretending that these] are the Emperor's commands, and that they [themselves] are merely acting as the Emperor's obedient Christian princes,[6] as if they meant it seriously and as if people were incapable of seeing through that sort of subterfuge. If the Emperor were to take away one of their castles or towns, or to command something else that did not seem right to them, we would soon see them finding reasons why they were entitled to resist and disobey him. But as long as it is a question of harassing the poor man and subjecting God's will to their own arbitrary whims, it must be called 'obedience to the Emperor's commands'. In days gone by, people like that were called scoundrels, but now we are to call them 'Christian and obedient princes'. And yet they will allow no one to obtain a hearing or to reply to charges against them, however humbly you plead with them, even though they would think it intolerable to be treated in that way themselves, by the Emperor or anyone else. These

---

[3] *An den Christlichen Adel deutscher Nation (Appeal to the Christian Nobility of the German Nation)*, 1520.

[4] Luther is referring to the demand of certain Catholic rulers that their subjects surrender their copies of Luther's German translation of the Bible.

[5] Or faith; the German word *Glaube* has both meanings.

[6] Luther's expression here is very crabbed. 'Obedient Christian princes' is in the original; Luther's term *Fürst* does not necessarily mean a 'sovereign'.

are the princes that rule the German territories of the Empire,[7] and it is little wonder that things there are in such a state.

Now, because the raging of these fools tends to the destruction of Christian faith, the denial of God's Word and blasphemy against God's majesty, I can no longer stand idly by and merely watch my ungracious lords and angry princes. I must resist them, even if it is only with words. And since I was not afraid of their idol the pope when he threatened me with the loss of heaven and my soul, I must show the world that I am not afraid of the pope's lackeys[8] either, who threaten me [only] with the loss of my life and worldly possessions. May God let them rage to the end of time[9] and help us to survive their threats. Amen.

1. Our first task is [to find] a firm grounding for secular law and the Sword,[10] in order to remove any possible doubt about their being in the world as a result of God's will and ordinance. The passages [of Scripture] which provide that foundation are these: Romans, 12 [in fact 13.1–2]: 'Let every soul be subject [363:] to power* and superiority*. For there is no power but from God and the power that exists everywhere is ordained by God. And whoever resists the power, resists God's ordinance. But whosoever resists God's ordinance shall receive condemnation on himself.'[11] And again 1 Peter 2 [13–14]: 'Be subject to every kind of human order, whether it be to the king as the foremost, or governors as sent by him, as a vengeance on the wicked and a reward to the just*.'

The Sword and its law have existed from the beginning of the world. When Cain beat his brother Abel to death, he was terrified that he would be killed in turn. But God imposed a special prohibition, suspending [punishment by] the sword for Cain's sake: no one was to

[7] The territories subject nominally or in fact to the Holy Roman Emperor at that time also included Spanish, Italian and Burgundian as well as German and Austrian territories, so Luther seems to be making a distinction.

[8] Literally: 'his scales' (the Devil was often depicted as having scales or plates like a fish or crocodile; see the passage on Leviathan in Job 41, normally interpreted as referring to the Devil) 'and waterbubbles': this is a play on words of which 'and all his bull' might be a faint imitation; the Latin word *bulla* literally means a bubble, the reference being to the seal. Luther found this pun irresistible.

[9] Literally: 'until the grey-coats (ie. monks' habits) vanish', apparently an idiom.

[10] For Luther's use of the metaphor of the Sword, see the Introduction, p. xvi.

[11] *Ordnung* may mean an ordinance or an order. The translation of this crucial text which Luther offers here is not that of his later versions in his German Bible. The word I have here translated as 'power' (*Gewalt*) he later rendered as *Oberkeit*, in later German this became *Obrigkeit*. Cf. Introduction, p. xv, and Glossary: power.

kill him. The only possible reason why Cain should have been afraid is that he had seen and heard from Adam that murderers should be killed. Furthermore, God re-instituted and confirmed [this command] in express words after the Flood when he says in Genesis 9 [6]: 'Whosoever sheds man's blood, by man let his blood be shed.' This cannot be interpreted as a reference to God [himself] inflicting suffering and punishment on murderers, since many of them, either because they repent or by favour, remain alive and die [naturally] without the sword. No: it refers to the right* of the Sword: a murderer forfeits his life, and it is right* that he should be killed by the sword. And if something prevents the law* being enforced, or if the sword is dilatory and the murderer dies a natural death, that does not prove Scripture wrong. What Scripture says is that whosoever sheds man's blood, that person's blood ought to be shed by men. It is the fault of men if God's law is not carried out, just as other commandments of God are not obeyed either.

The Law of Moses afterwards confirmed this [command]: 'If a man should kill his neighbour out of malice, him shall you drag from my altar, to kill him' (Exodus 21 [14]). And again: 'A life for a life, an eye for an eye, a tooth for a tooth, a foot for a foot, a hand for a hand, a wound for a wound, a bruise for a bruise.' And what is more, Christ too confirms it when he said to Peter in the garden [of Gethsemane, Matt. 26.52]: 'Whoever takes up the sword shall perish by the sword', which is to be understood in the same sense as Genesis 9[6]: 'Whoever sheds man's blood etc.'; there is no doubt that Christ is here invoking those words, and wishes to have this commandment introduced and confirmed [in the New Covenant]. John the Baptist teaches the same [Luke 3.14]. When the soldiers asked him what they were to do, he told them: 'Do no violence* or injustice to anyone and be content with your pay.' If the Sword were not an occupation[12] approved by God, John ought to have commanded them to cease to be soldiers, all the more since [his vocation] was to make the people perfect and to teach them in a true [364:] Christian manner. How the secular Sword and law are to be employed according to God's will is thus clear and certain enough: to punish the wicked and protect the just*.

2. But what Christ says in Matthew 5 [38–9] sounds as if it were

---

[12] Literally 'estate'; cf. Glossary. For Luther's thinking about the morality of soldiering, cf. for example: *Ob Kriegsleute auch im seeligen Stand sein könnten (Whether Soldiers too can be in a State of Grace)*, 1526.

emphatically opposed to this: 'You have heard what was said to your ancestors: an eye for an eye, a tooth for a tooth. But I say to you: resist no evil. Rather, if anyone strikes you on the right cheek, turn him the other cheek. And if someone will dispute with you at law, to take your coat, let him have your cloak also. And if a man should compel you to go with him one mile, go two miles etc.' To the same effect, Paul in Romans 12 [19]: 'Dearly beloved, do not defend yourselves, but rather give place unto the wrath of God. For it is written: Vengeance is mine; I will repay, says the Lord.' And again, Matthew 5 [44]: 'Love your enemies. Do good unto them that hate you.' And 1 Peter 2 [error for 3.9]: 'No one shall render evil for evil, or insults for insults etc.' These and others of the same sort are hard sayings, and sound as if Christians in the New Covenant were to have no secular Sword.

This is why the sophists say that Christ has abolished the Law of Moses, and why they make [mere] 'counsels of perfection' out of such commands. They then divide up Christian doctrine and the Christian estate* into two parts. The one part they call 'those who are perfect', and to this they allot the 'counsels'; the other part they term 'the imperfect' and to them they allot the commands. But this is pure effrontery and wilfulness, without any warrant from Scripture. They fail to notice that in that very place Christ imposes his teachings so emphatically, that he will not have the slightest thing removed from it, and condemns to hell those who do not love their enemies [Matt. 5.22ff]. We must therefore interpret him in another way, so that his words continue to apply to all, be they 'perfect' or 'imperfect'. For perfection and imperfection do not inhere in works, and do not establish any distinction in outward condition or status* between Christians; rather, they inhere in the heart, in faith, in love, so that whoever believes more [firmly] and loves more, that person is perfect, irrespective of whether it be a man or a woman, a prince or a peasant, monk or layman. For love and faith create no factions and no outward distinctions.

3. Here we must divide Adam's children, all mankind, into two parts: the first belong to the kingdom* of God, the second to the kingdom of the world*. All those who truly believe in Christ belong to God's kingdom, for Christ is king and lord in God's kingdom, as the second Psalm [v. 6] and the whole of Scripture proclaims. And Christ came in order to begin the kingdom of God and to establish it in the world. This is why he said before Pilate [John 18.36ff]: 'My kingdom is not [365:]

8

of this world, but whoever belongs to the truth hears my voice', and why throughout the Gospel he announces the kingdom of God, saying [Matt. 3.2]: 'Repent, for the kingdom of God is at hand'; and again [Matt. 6.33]: 'Seek first the kingdom of God and its righteousness.' And indeed he calls the Gospel a gospel of the kingdom of God, in that it teaches, governs and preserves the kingdom of God.

Now: these people need neither secular [*weltlich*]* Sword nor law*. And if all the world [*Welt*] were true Christians, that is, if everyone truly believed, there would be neither need nor use for princes, kings, lords, the Sword or law. What would there be for them to do? Seeing that [true Christians] have the Holy Spirit in their hearts, which teaches and moves them to love everyone, wrong no one, and suffer wrongs gladly, even unto death. Where all wrongs are endured willingly and what is right* is done freely, there is no place for quarrelling, disputes, courts, punishments, laws or the Sword. And therefore laws and the secular Sword cannot possibly find any work to do among Christians, especially since they of themselves do much more than any laws or teachings might demand. As Paul says in 1 Tim. 1 [9]: 'Laws are not given to the just, but to the unjust.'

Why should this be? It is because the just man [*der Gerechte*] of his own accord does all and more than any law* [*Recht*] demands. But the unjust [*Ungerechten*] do nothing that is right [*recht*], and therefore they need the law to teach, compel and urge them to act rightly. A good tree[13] needs no teaching and no law in order for it to bear good fruit; it is its nature to do so without teaching or law. A man would have to be an idiot to write a book of laws for an apple-tree telling it to bear apples and not thorns, seeing that the apple-tree will do it naturally and far better than any laws or teaching can prescribe. In the same way, because of the spirit and faith, the nature of all Christians is such that they act well and rightly, better than any laws can teach them, and therefore they have no need of any laws for themselves.

You will reply: 'Why then has God given all mankind so many laws and why has Christ in the Gospel taught so much about what we ought to do?' I have written at length about this in my 'Postil'[14] and elsewhere and therefore I shall state the matter very briefly. St Paul says that the law is given for the sake of the unjust. In other words, those who are not

---

[13] The implicit reference is to the parable in Matthew 7.18.
[14] i.e. *Sermons on the Church's Year*; cf. Weimar edition, 10:2:152–70.

Christians are constrained by laws to refrain outwardly from wicked deeds, as we shall see below. But since no man is by nature a Christian or just,[15] but all are sinners and evil, God hinders them all, by means of the law, from doing as they please and expressing their wickedness outwardly in actions. [366:] And St Paul assigns another task to the law[16] in Romans 7[7], and Galatians 2 [in fact 3.19 and 24]: it teaches how sin may be recognized, so as to humble man into a willingness to accept grace and faith in Christ. Christ teaches the same in Matthew 5[39]: evil is not to be resisted. Here he is explaining the law and is teaching us the nature of a true Christian, as we shall hear below.

4. All those who are not Christians [in the above sense] belong to the kingdom of the world* or [in other words] are under the law. There are few who believe, and even fewer who behave like Christians and refrain from doing evil [themselves], let alone not resisting evil [done to them]. And for the rest God has established another government,[17] outside the Christian estate* and the kingdom* of God, and has cast them into subjection to the Sword. So that, however much they would like to do evil, they are unable to act in accordance with their inclinations, or, if they do, they cannot do so without fear, or enjoy peace and good fortune. In the same way, a wicked, fierce animal is chained and bound so that it cannot bite or tear, as its nature would prompt it to do, however much it wants to; whereas a tame, gentle animal needs nothing like chains or bonds and is harmless even without them.

If there were [no law and government], then seeing that all the world is evil and that scarcely one human being in a thousand is a true Christian, people would devour each other and no one would be able to support his wife and children, feed himself and serve God. The world* [*Welt*] would become a desert. And so God has ordained the two

---

[15] *Fromm*; cf. Glossary: just. Note that Luther's German here is ambiguous, more so than some commentators allow. He does not say that no one in the world is a Christian or just, merely that no one is so 'naturally', which may mean either that some are both, but by divine grace alone, or it may mean, as commentators would like it to mean, that Christians in their outward conduct remain imperfect. It is not in the least obvious that Luther meant the latter, and the lack of clarity is significant, given Luther's previous bipartite division of the human race, and his insistence that it is 'Christians', and not human beings to the extent that they actually behave like Christians, who need no sword or law. In the next few pages, his point is the paucity of true Christians.

[16] Here and in the previous sentence Luther appears to mean the Ten Commandments, but he has not explicitly distinguished between man-made, positive law and divine law.

[17] Luther is here distinguishing between 'kingdom' (*Reich*) and 'government' (*Regiment*). For the content and implications of this distinction, see the Glossary, pp. xxxv–xxxvi.

governments*, the spiritual [government] which fashions true Christians and just persons through the Holy Spirit under Christ, and the secular* [*weltlich*] government which holds the Unchristian and wicked in check and forces them to keep the peace outwardly and be still, like it or not. It is in this way that St Paul interprets the secular Sword when he says in Romans 13[3]: 'It [the Sword] is not a terror to good works, but to the wicked.' And Peter says [1 Pet. 2.14]: 'It is given as a punishment on the wicked.'

If someone wanted to have the world* ruled according to the Gospel, and to abolish all secular* law and the Sword, on the ground that all are baptized and Christians and that the Gospel will have no law or sword used among Christians, who have no need of them [in any case], what do you imagine the effect would be? He would let loose the wild animals from their bonds and chains, and let them maul and tear everyone to pieces, saying all the while that really they are just fine, tame, gentle, little things. But my wounds would tell me different. And so the wicked under cover of the name of Christians, would misuse the freedom of the Gospel, would work their wickedness and would claim that they are Christians and [therefore] subject to no law and no Sword. Some of them are raving like this already.[18]

[367:] Such a person must be told that it is of course true that Christians are subject to neither the law nor the Sword for their own sake, and do not need them. But before you rule the world in the Christian and Gospel manner, be sure to fill it with true Christians. And that you will never do, because the world and the many are unchristian and will remain so, whether they are made up of baptized and nominal Christians or not. But Christians, as the saying goes, are few and far between, and the world will not tolerate a Christian government* ruling over one land or a great multitude, let alone over the whole world. There are always many more of the wicked than there are of the just*. And so to try to rule a whole country or the world by means of the Gospel is like herding together wolves, lions, eagles and sheep in the same pen, letting them mix freely, and saying to them: feed, and be just and peaceable; the stable isn't locked, there's plenty of pasture, and you have no dogs or cudgels to be afraid of. The sheep

---

[18] The reference appears to be to Anabaptists. Compare his *Wider die Himmlischen Propheten (Against the Heavenly Prophets)*. He was shortly to make much the same complaints against the rebellious peasants. See *Wider die Räuberischen Mörderischen Rotten (Against the Thieving, Murdering Hordes of Peasants)*, 1525.

would certainly keep the peace and let themselves be governed and pastured peaceably, but they would not live long.

Therefore care must be taken to keep these two governments* distinct, and both must be allowed to continue [their work], the one to make [people] just*, the other to create outward peace and prevent evil-doing. Neither is enough for the world without the other. Without the spiritual government of Christ, no one can be made just in the sight of God by the secular government [alone]. However, Christ's spiritual government does not extend to everyone; on the contrary, Christians are at all times the fewest in number and live in the midst of the Unchristian. Conversely, where the secular government or law rules on its own, pure hypocrisy must prevail, even if it were God's own commandments [that were being enforced]. For no one becomes truly just without the Holy Spirit in his heart, however good his works.[19] And equally where the spiritual government rules over a country and its people unaided, every sort of wickedness is let loose and every sort of knavery has free play. For the world in general is incapable of accepting it or understanding it [i.e. the spiritual government].

You can now see the implication of the words of Christ which we cited earlier from Matthew 5 [39], that Christians are not to go to law or use the secular Sword amongst themselves. This is really only said to the Christians he loves, and it is only they that accept it and act accordingly, rather than reducing it to mere 'counsels', like the sophists. On the contrary, such is the character that the Holy Spirit has imparted to their hearts, that they do harm to no one, but rather suffer it willingly at the hands of anyone else. Now if all the world were Christian, these words would apply to them all and they would all act accordingly. But since they are unchristian, the words have nothing to do with them, and neither do they follow them. Instead they belong under the other [i.e. secular] government, by which the Unchristian are outwardly constrained and forced to behave peaceably and well.

[368:] For the same reason Christ did not bear the Sword [in person], or institute it in his kingdom: he is king over Christians and rules by his Holy Spirit alone, without any laws. And even though he confirmed [the legitimacy of] the Sword, he himself made no use of it,

---

[19] The reference is to Luther's core doctrine of justification by faith alone: such is human depravity since the Fall that no human being can behave so correctly and will what is right by his own unaided efforts (works) as to deserve God's rewards as of right. cf. *Von den Guten Werken (On Good Works)*, 1520.

for it does not advance his kingdom, which contains none but the just. It is for this same reason that in the old days David was not permitted to build the Temple, for he had borne the Sword and shed much blood. Not that he had done wrong thereby, but he could not prefigure Christ, who will have a peaceful kingdom without the Sword. Instead, Solomon must do it – 'Solomon' in German means peaceable, peaceful[20] – for Solomon had a peaceful kingdom, which could therefore be the emblem of the peaceful kingdom of Christ, the true Solomon. And again, during the whole time the Temple was built, says the Scripture, there was heard no sound of iron; all this because Christ wanted a free, willing people without coercion or constraint, law or Sword [1 Kings 6.7].

This is what is meant by the prophets: Psalm 109 [possibly Ps. 110.3]: 'Thy people shall be those who are willing', and Isaiah 11[9]: 'They shall not kill or harm on all my holy mountain' (in other words the Church). And Isaiah 2[4]: 'They shall make their swords into ploughshares and their spears into sickles; and no one shall raise a sword against another; and they shall study fighting no more etc.' Those who want to extend the meaning of these and similar sayings to make them cover all who call themselves Christians would be perverting [the meaning of] Scripture, for these things are said only of the true Christians, who do in fact act in this way towards each other.

5.   You will object here: seeing that Christians need neither the secular Sword nor law, why does Paul in Romans 13[1] say to all Christians: 'Let every soul be subject to power* and superiority*'?[21] And St Peter [1 Pet. 2.13]: 'Be subject to every human ordinance etc.', as cited above? My answer is: I have already said that Christians among themselves and for themselves need no law and no Sword, for they have no use for them. But because a true Christian, while he is on the earth, lives for and serves his neighbour and not himself, he does things that are of no benefit to himself, but of which his neighbour stands in need. Such is the nature of the Christian's spirit. Now the Sword is indispensable for the whole world, to preserve peace, punish sin, and restrain the wicked. And therefore Christians readily submit them-

---

[20] Luther here refers, by implication, to the fact that etymologically the German name Friedrich is identical to the Hebrew name Solomon. Since the reference is untranslatable, I have suppressed it. I suspect a flattering allusion to Frederick the Wise, Elector of Saxony and Luther's patron.
[21] Cf. fn. 11 above.

selves to be governed by the Sword, they pay taxes, honour those in authority*, serve and help them, and do what they can to uphold their power, so that they may continue their work, and that honour and fear of authority may be maintained. [All this] even though Christians do not need it for themselves [369:], but they attend to what others need, as Paul teaches in Ephesians 5[21].

In the same way, the Christian performs every other work of love that he does not require for himself. He visits the sick, but not in order to become well himself. He does not feed others because he needs food for himself. And neither does he serve authority* because he himself stands in need of it, but because others do, in order that they might enjoy protection, and so that the wicked might not grow even worse. Such service* does no harm to him, and he suffers no loss by it, but the world benefits greatly. To omit to do it would not be the act of a Christian; it would be contrary to [the Christian duty of] love, and would give a bad example to [the Unchristian]: they too would refuse to submit to authority, although they are unchristian. And all this would bring the Gospel into disrepute, as if it taught rebellion and created selfish people unwilling to be of use or service to anyone, whereas the Gospel makes the Christian a servant to everyone. Thus Christ in Matthew 17[27] paid the tax, although he had no need to do so, in order not to give offence.

And so in the words quoted above from Matthew 5[39], you do indeed find Christ teaching that those who are his are to have no secular Sword or law among themselves. But he does not forbid them to serve and be subject to those who do have the secular Sword and laws. On the contrary, precisely because you do not need it and are not to have it, you ought to serve those who have not reached the same [spiritual] level as you and do still need it. Although you yourself do not need your enemy to be punished, your weak neighbour does, and you are to help him to enjoy peace and to see to it that his enemies are kept in check. And that cannot be unless power* and superiors* are held in honour and awe. The words of Christ are *not*: you are not to serve the power, nor be subject to it; but rather: 'you shall not resist evil', as if to say: so conduct yourself as to suffer all things, so that you have no need for those in power* to help or serve or be of use to you; on the contrary, *you* are to help, serve and be indispensable to them. I will have you be of such a noble and honourable status as not to need them; rather they shall need you.

6. You ask whether a Christian can even wield the secular Sword and punish the wicked [himself], seeing that Christ's words 'Do not resist evil' seem so peremptory and clear that the sophists have to water them down into a mere 'counsel'. Answer, 'you have now heard two [conflicting] things. One is that there can be no Sword amongst Christians. And therefore you cannot bear the Sword over or among Christians. So the question is irrelevant in that context and must instead be asked in connection with the other group [the Unchristian]: can a Christian use be made of it with regard to them? This is [370:] where the second part [of what I have said] applies, the one that says that you owe the Sword your service and support, by whatever means are available to you, be it with your body, goods, honour or soul. For this is a work of which you yourself have no need, but your neighbour and the whole world most certainly do. And therefore if you see that there is a lack of hangmen, court officials, judges, lords or princes, and you find that you have the necessary skills, then you should offer your services and seek office, so that authority*, which is so greatly needed, will never come to be held in contempt, become powerless, or perish. The world cannot get by without it.

How does this resolve the difficulty? In this way: all such actions would be devoted wholly to the service* of others; they would benefit only your neighbour and not you or your possessions and honour. You would not be aiming at revenge [for yourself], at repaying evil with evil, but rather at the good of your neighbours, the preservation, protection and peace of others. As far as you yourself and your possessions are concerned, you keep to the Gospel and act according to Christ's word; you would gladly turn the other cheek and give up your cloak as well as your coat, when it is you and your possessions that are involved. And so the two are nicely reconciled: you satisfy the demands of God's kingdom* and the world's at one and the same time, outwardly and inwardly; you both suffer evil and injustice and yet punish them; you do not resist evil and yet you do resist it. For you attend to yourself and what is yours in one way, and to your neighbour and what is his in another. As to you and yours, you keep to the Gospel and suffer injustice as a true Christian. But where the next man and what is his are concerned, you act in accordance with the [command to] love and you tolerate no injustice against him. And that is not prohibited by the Gospel; on the contrary the Gospel commands it elsewhere [cf Romans 13:4].

It is in this way that all the saints have borne the Sword from the beginning of the world: Adam and his descendants, Abraham when he saved Lot, his brother's son, and slew the four kings (Genesis 14[13–16]); and surely Abraham typifies the whole Gospel? This is how the holy prophet Samuel slew King Agag (1 Samuel 15[32ff]) and Elias the prophets of Baal (1 Kings 18[40]). And Moses, Joshua, the Children of Israel, Samson, David and all the kings and princes of the Old Testament acted in the same way. So did Daniel and his companions Ananias, Asarias and Mishael in Babylon; so did Joseph in Egypt and so forth.

Some would claim here that the Old Covenant is abolished and no longer valid and that there is therefore no point in rehearsing these examples to Christians. Not so. For St Paul says in 1 Corinthians 10[3]: 'They have eaten the same spiritual food as we, and have drunk the same spiritual drink from the rock which is Christ.' That is: they had the same spirit and faith in Christ that we have [371:], and were just as much Christians as we are. And what it was right for them to do is right for all Christians, from the beginning to the end of the world. For time and outward changes make no difference among Christians. Nor is it true that the Old Covenant has been abolished, so that it need not be kept, or that it is wrong to keep it – a point on which St Jerome and many others have slipped up. Rather, this is the way in which the Old Covenant has been abolished: doing or omitting are left free, and no longer bind on pain of losing our souls, as they did formerly.

For St Paul says in 1 Corinthians 7[19] and Galatians 6[15]: 'Neither uncircumcision nor circumcision are anything; rather: a new creation in Christ.' That is: it is no sin to be uncircumcised, [contrary to what] the Jews thought, neither is it a sin to be circumcised, as the pagans thought, but both are equally good and equally left to our discretion, as long as whoever does them does not think he will be justified* or saved thereby. The same is true of all the other parts of the Old Covenant: it is neither wrong to omit, nor wrong to do, but everything is left as free and good, to be done or omitted. And in fact, were it a question of what is necessary or conducive to the salvation of our neighbour's soul, it would be obligatory to keep them all. Everyone has a duty to do what is necessary for his neighbour, irrespective of whether it is under the Old or the New Covenant, be it something Jewish or pagan, as St Paul teaches in 1 Corinthians 12[13]: 'Love penetrates everything and transcends everything, and looks only to the need and advantage of

others, but does not ask whether it is old or new.' The same goes for the
examples of the [use of the] Sword. You are free to follow them or not.
But when you see your neighbour in need, then love obliges you to do
what would otherwise be left free to do or omit. Only do not imagine
that your actions will justify or save you, as the Jews had the audacity to
think; rather leave that to faith, which makes you into a new creation
without works.[22]

But to prove my point from the New Testament as well, we can rely
on John the Baptist (Luke 3[15]), whose duty was without a doubt to
witness to, show forth, and teach Christ; that is, his doctrine was to be
evangelical, the pure New Testament, and he was to lead a perfect
people to Christ. John confirms the office of soldier, saying that they
are to be content with their pay. If it were unchristian to bear the sword,
he should have punished them and told them to throw away both their
swords and their pay; otherwise he would not have been teaching them
what is fitting for Christians. And when St Peter in Acts 10[34ff] was
teaching Cornelius about Christ, he did not tell him to abandon his
office, as he should have done if it had been a hindrance to Cornelius'
[attaining] the status* of a Christian. [372:] Furthermore, before [Cor-
nelius] was baptized [Acts 10.44], the Holy Spirit descended on him.
And St Luke praised him as a just man [Acts 10.2] before Peter taught
him, and did not find fault with him for being a commander of soldiers
and a captain of the pagan Emperor. What it was right for the Holy
Spirit to leave unchanged and unpunished in Cornelius is equally right
for us.

The same example is given to us by the Ethiopian eunuch, a captain,
in Acts 8[27ff], whom the evangelist Philip converted and baptized and
then allowed to retain his office and return home. [The Ethiopian]
could hardly have held such a powerful office under the Queen of
Ethiopia without bearing the sword. The same is true of the Governor
of Cyprus, Sergius Paulus (Acts 13[7,12]), whom St Paul converted
and yet allowed to remain governor among and over pagans. And the
same was done by many holy martyrs, who were obedient to the pagan
emperors of Rome, went into battle under them and no doubt killed
people to keep the peace, as is written of St Maurice, St Achatius and
St Gereon, and of many others under the Emperor Julian [the
Apostate].[23]

[22] Cf. fn. 19 above.
[23] Luther is here using illustrations from the popular legends of the Old Church.

But more important than all these is the clear, strong text (Romans 13[1]), where St Paul says: 'Power* is the ordinance of God.' And again: 'Those in power do not bear the sword in vain. For power is the handmaiden of God, his avenger for your good against him that does evil' [Romans 13.4]. My dear brother, do not presume to say that the Christian must not do what is in fact God's own work, ordinance and creation. Otherwise you would also have to say that the Christian must not eat, drink, or marry, for these too are God's works and ordinances. And since they are, they are good, and equally it is good for everyone to make a Christian use of them, as St Paul says in 2 Timothy 4[4]: 'Everything created by God is good, and not to be rejected by the faithful and those who recognize the truth.' And you must count not only food and drink, clothes and shoes, but also power and subordination, protection and punishment, as things created by God.

So to cut a long story short: because St Paul says that power is the handmaiden of God, its use must be allowed not only to pagans but to all mankind. For what can it mean to say that power is the handmaiden of God, if not that it is by nature something which can be used to serve God. It would be wholly unchristian to say that there is anything which serves God and which yet a Christian should not do, for there is no one more suited to serving God than a Christian. In the same way it is right and necessary that all princes [373:] should be good Christians. The Sword and power, as a special service* rendered to God, are more suited to Christians than to anyone else in the world, and so you should value the Sword and power as much as the married state, or cultivating the soil, or any other trade instituted by God. Just as a man can serve God in the married state, in farming or manual labour, for the benefit of his neighbour, and indeed must do so if his neighbour's need demands it, so too he can serve God by the [exercise of] power, and he ought to do it, when his neighbour needs it. For those are God's servants and labourers who punish evil and protect what is good. But this is to be left to free choice where there is no [absolute] need, just as marrying and engaging in farming are also left to people's choice, where there is no [absolute] need.

If you then ask: why did Christ and the Apostles not exercise power? my answer is: why did not [Christ] take a wife, or become a cobbler or tailor? Are we to think that a status* or occupation* is not good merely because Christ did not have it himself? In that case, what would happen to every status and occupation except that of preacher, since that was the only one he held? Christ occupied the office and status* proper to him, but in doing so he did not condemn any other. It was not fitting for him to bear the Sword, for his only office was to be that of ruling his kingdom and whatever serves that kingdom alone. And it did not pertain to his kingship* to become a husband, cobbler, tailor, plough-man, prince, hangman, or beadle; nor again to bear the Sword or [make] secular laws; all that did pertain to it was God's Word and spirit by which his own are governed, inwardly. And the office he held then and continues to hold now is always bestowed by the spirit and God's Word. And the apostles and all spiritual governors were to succeed him in that office. That work, the work of the spiritual Sword, the Word of God, will give them so much to do, if they are to do it properly, that they will have to neglect the secular Sword and leave it to others who do not have to attend to preaching, even though it is not incompatible with their status to do so,[24] as has been said. For everyone must attend to his own calling* and work.

And so, even though Christ did not bear or teach[25] the Sword himself, it is enough that he did not forbid or abolish it but rather confirmed it, just as it is enough that he did not abolish the married state but confirmed it, albeit he himself took no wife and taught nothing about it. For the task appropriate to his status* was to concern himself wholly with that work which specifically served his kingdom and nothing else, to prevent his example being treated as a binding reason for teaching and believing that God's kingdom could not continue without marriage or the Sword [374:] or suchlike outward things, whereas that kingdom subsists by God's Word and spirit alone. (For Christ's example compels imitation.) Christ's own office* was and had to be that of the most high king in this same kingdom. And since not all Christians have the same office (even though they could have it), it is right and fitting that they should have some other external [office], by which God may also be served.

From all this it follows that the right interpretation of Christ's words in Matthew 5[39]: 'You shall not resist evil etc.' is that Christians should be capable of suffering every evil and injustice, not avenging

---

[24] Luther's expression here is sense-destroyingly elliptical. I think what is meant is some-thing like: 'It is not against the minister's status as a Christian to wield secular authority, but against his particular vocation. For . . .'.

[25] I think this means: 'or teach others how to exercise coercive authority'. Note how completely the metaphorical Sword has become dissociated in Luther's mind from the physical sword.

themselves, and not going to court in self-defence either. On the contrary they will require nothing at all for themselves from secular authority and laws [*Recht*]*. But they may seek retribution, justice [*Recht*], protection and help for others, and do whatever they want to that end. And those in power* for their part should help and protect them, either on their own initiative, or at the behest of others, even though the Christians themselves lodge no complaint, and do not petition or institute proceedings. Where [the secular authorities] fail to do so, the Christian should allow himself to be abused and maltreated, and should not resist evil, just as Christ's Word says.

But you may be sure of this: this teaching of Christ is not a 'counsel for the perfect', as our blaspheming and lying sophists will have it, but a strict injunction to every Christian. And rest assured that those who avenge themselves and litigate and quarrel in the courts for their goods and honour are mere pagans bearing the name of Christians, and will never be anything else. Pay no attention to the common run of people and what they usually do. Make no mistake about it: there are few Christians on earth. And God's command is something different from what is usually done.

You can see here that Christ did not abolish the Law when he said: 'You have heard how it was said to your ancestors: an eye for an eye. But I say to you: you shall not resist evil etc.' [Matthew 5.38f]. Rather, he is interpreting the meaning of the Law and telling us how it ought to be understood, as if to say: you Jews think that it is right and proper in the sight of God for you to recover what is yours by [recourse to] the law, and you rely on Moses saying 'an eye for an eye etc.' But I say to you that Moses gave this law on account of the wicked, who do not belong to God's kingdom, to prevent them from taking revenge themselves or doing worse. By such externally imposed law they would be compelled to desist from evil, and would be hedged about by outward law and government, and subjected to authority*. But you are so to conduct yourselves that you neither need nor seek such law. For although secular authority must have such laws, to judge the unbelieving, and even though you yourselves may make use of it to judge others, all the same for yourselves and in your own affairs you are neither [375:] to resort to it nor to use it, for you have the kingdom of heaven and you should leave the earthly kingdom [*Erdreich*] to those who take it from you.

You see, then, that Christ did not interpret his [own] words as abolishing the Law of Moses or as prohibiting secular authority. Rather he withdraws those who are his own from it, so that they will make no use of it for themselves, but leave it for the unbelievers, whom they may indeed serve with such laws, since the Unchristian do exist, and no one can be made a true Christian by compulsion. But it becomes clear that Christ's words are directed to his alone when he says somewhat later that they are to love their enemies and to be perfect, as their heavenly father is perfect [Matt. 5.44,48]. But a man who is perfect and loves his enemy, leaves the law behind; he does not need it to exact an eye for an eye. But neither does he hinder the Unchristian who do not love their enemy and who do want to employ the law; on the contrary, he helps the law to catch the wicked, to prevent them doing still more wickedness.

This, in my view, is how the words of Christ are reconciled with those texts that institute the Sword. What they mean is that Christians are neither to employ nor to call on the Sword for themselves and in their own concerns. But they may and should use it and call on it for the sake of others, so that evil may be prevented and justice upheld. In just the same way the Lord says in the same place that Christians shall not take oaths, but that their speech is to be yea, yea and nay, nay [Matt. 5.34ff]. In other words, they are not to take oaths on their own behalf or of their own will and inclination. But when the necessity, benefit and salvation [of others] or the honour of God demands it, they should take oaths. They make use of the [otherwise] forbidden oath to help others, in precisely the same way that they use the prohibited sword. Indeed Christ and Paul themselves often swear on oath, in order to make their teaching and witness beneficial and credible to mankind, as people do, and are allowed to do, in those treaties and compacts of which the 62nd Psalm [in fact 63 v. 12] speaks: 'They are praised, who swear by his name.'

A further question that arises is whether beadles, hangmen, lawyers, advocates and all the rest of their sort can be Christians and in a state* of grace? The answer is that if government [*die Gewalt*]* and the Sword serve God, as has been shown above, then everything that government needs in order to bear the Sword, is equally a service to God. There has to be someone to catch the wicked, to accuse them, and execute them, and to protect, acquit, defend and save the good. And therefore if the intention of those who carry out these tasks is not that of looking to their own advantage, but only of helping to uphold the laws and authorities, in order to repress the wicked, then there is no danger in it for them, and they can do it like any other job, [376:] and get their living by it. As has already been said, love of one's neighbour has no regard for self, neither does it consider whether what is to be done is important or trivial, so long as it is for the good of one's neighbour or the community*.[26]

Finally, you might ask: can't I use the Sword for myself and my own concerns, provided I am not out for my own good, but merely intend that evil should be punished? My answer is that such a miracle is not impossible, but very unusual and dangerous.[27] It may happen where the Spirit is present in great fulness. We do indeed read in Judges 15[11] that Samson said: 'I have done unto them as they did unto me.' But against this is Proverbs 24[29]: 'Do not say: I will do unto him, as he has done unto me.' And Proverbs 20[22]: 'Do not say: I will repay his wickedness.' Samson was required by God to plague the Philistines and save the children of Israel. And even though he used his private concerns as a pretext for declaring war against them, he nevertheless did not do it to avenge himself or to seek his own advantage, but to help [the Israelites] and punish the Philistines. But no one can follow this precedent unless he be a true Christian, filled with the [Holy] Spirit. Where [ordinary human] reason wants to do likewise, it no doubt pretends that it is not seeking its own advantage, but the claim will be false from top to bottom. The thing is impossible without grace. So if you want to act like Samson, then first become like Samson.

Part Two

How far secular authority extends

We now come to the main part of this sermon. We have learnt that there must be secular authority on this earth and how a Christian and salutary use may be made of it. Now we must establish how long its reach is, and how far it may stretch out its arm without overreaching itself and trenching upon God's kingdom* and government. This is something about which we need to be quite clear. When [secular government] is given too much freedom of action, the harm that results is unbearable and horrifying, but to have it confined within too narrow a compass is

---

[26] *Gemeine* (= *Gemeinde*), Luther's generic term for a human collectivity, be it a congregation, parish, city or polity.

[27] Another crabbed sentence: the meaning is, I take it, such a thing is not impossible, but so rare as to be almost a miracle, and it is dangerous to act in this way.

also harmful. In the one case there is too much punishment, in the other too little. But it is more tolerable to err on the side of the latter: it is always better that a villain should live than that a just* man should be killed. There always are, and always must be, villains in the world, but there are few just men.

[377:] The first point to be noted is that the two parts into which the children of Adam are divided (as we have said above), the one the kingdom of God* under Christ, the other the kingdom of the world* under [secular] authority*, have each their own kind of law*. Everyday experience sufficiently shows us that every kingdom must have its own laws and that no kingdom or government can survive without law. Secular government has laws that extend no further than the body, goods and outward, earthly* matters. But where the soul is concerned, God neither can nor will allow anyone but himself to rule. And so, where secular authority takes it upon itself to legislate for the soul, it trespasses on [what belongs to] God's government, and merely seduces and ruins souls. I intend to make this so unambiguously clear that no one can fail to grasp it, in order that our lords the princes and bishops may see the folly of trying to compel belief in this or that by means of laws and commands.

If someone imposes a man-made law on souls, compelling belief in what he wants to be believed, then there will probably be no word of God to justify it.[28] If there is nothing in God's Word about it, then it is uncertain whether this is what God wants. If he himself has not commanded something, there is no way of establishing that it is pleasing to him. Or rather, we can be sure that it is not pleasing to him, for he will have our faith grounded solely in his divine Word; as he says in Matthew 18 [in fact 16.18]: 'On this rock I will build my church.'[29] And John 10[27]: 'My sheep hear my voice and know me, but the strangers' voice they hear not, but flee from them.' From this it follows

---

[28] 'To justify it' is my deliberately ambiguous rendering of Luther's casual '*da*' (there), which may mean 'such a belief', or Luther may mean (as I suppose him to mean) that people will impose beliefs only when they cannot find scriptural warrant for the belief in question. In either case, Luther is equivocating on the question of the legitimacy of compelling professions of belief on matters on which Scripture *is* unambiguous.

[29] This text (for which Luther remarkably gave the wrong reference) is the *locus classicus* for underwriting papal authority and Luther is deliberately turning it into another direction: the 'rock', on this interpretation, is to be understood as faith, and not, as the text appears to say, as Peter. In the Greek and Hebrew, the words for 'Peter' and 'rock' are identical, in Latin almost.

that secular authority drives souls to eternal damnation with such blasphemous commands. For this is to compel people to believe that something is certain to please God, when it is not certain at all; on the contrary, it is certain that it displeases God, since there is no clear [text in] God's Word to warrant it. For whosoever believes something to be right, which is in fact wrong or uncertain, denies the truth, which is God himself, and believes lies and error . . .[30]

It is therefore utter folly for them to order us to believe the Church, the [Church] Fathers and the Councils, even though there is no [express] Word of God [for what they tell us to believe]. It is the apostles of the devil that issue that sort of command, not the Church. The Church commands nothing except what it is certain is God's Word. As St Peter says [1 Pet. 4.11]: 'Whoever speaks, let him speak according to God's word.' But they will never be able to show that the decrees of Councils are the Word of God. And what is even more ridiculous is when it is argued that, after all, this is what kings and princes and people generally believe. But, my friends, we are not baptized in the name of kings and princes and people in general, but in the name of Christ and of God himself. And our title is not 'kings' or 'princes' or 'people in general', but Christians. [378:] No one can or should lay down commandments for the soul, except those who can point it on the way to heaven. But no human being can do that; only God. And therefore in those things which concern the salvation of souls, nothing is to be taught or accepted except God's Word.

Another important point is this. However stupid they are, they must admit that they have no power over the soul. For no human being can kill the soul or bring it to life, or lead it to heaven or to hell. And if they will not believe us, then Christ will show it clearly enough when he says in Matthew 10[28]: 'Do not be afraid of those that kill the body and after that can do nothing more. Fear rather him who, after he kills the body, has the power to condemn to hell.' Surely that is clear enough: the soul is taken out of the hands of any human being whatsoever, and is placed exclusively under the power* of God. Now tell me this: would anyone in his right mind give orders where he has no authority*? You might as well command the moon to shine at your behest. What sense would there be in it, if the people of Leipzig were to lay down laws for us here in Wittenberg, or vice versa? Anyone who tried it, would be sent a

---

[30] The text continues pleonastically: 'holding that to be right [or just] which is wrong [or unjust, *unrecht*]'.

dose of hellebore by way of thanks, to clear their heads and cure their cold. But this is just what our Emperor[31] and our prudent princes are doing; they let the Pope, the bishops and the sophists lead them, the blind leading the blind, commanding their subjects to believe as they see fit, without God's Word. And then they still want to retain the title of 'Christian Princes', which God forbid.

Another way of understanding this point is that each and every authority can only act, and ought only to act, where it can see, know, judge, adjudicate and change things. What kind of judge would it be that judges blindly in matters where he can neither hear nor see? But tell me this: how can a human being see, know, judge and change hearts? That is reserved to God alone. As Psalm 7[10] says: 'God searches the heart and bowels.'[32] And again [Ps. 7.9]: 'The Lord is judge over the people', and Acts 10 [in fact 1.24; 15.8]: 'God knows the heart.' And Jeremiah 1 [in fact 17.9]: 'Wicked and unsearchable is the human heart. Who can search it? I the Lord, who search hearts and bowels.' A court has to have an exact knowledge of what it is to judge. But people's thoughts and minds cannot be manifest to anyone but God. And therefore it is impossible and futile to command or coerce someone to believe this or that. A different skill is needed here; force* will not do. I am surprised at these lunatics [379:], seeing that they themselves have a saying: *De occultis non iudicat ecclesia*; the Church does not judge in secret matters. Now, if [even] the Church, the spiritual government, only rules over matters that are public and open, by what right does secular authority, in its folly, presume to judge a thing as secret, spiritual, hidden as faith?

Each must decide at his own peril what he is to believe, and must see to it that he believes rightly. Other people cannot go to heaven or hell on my behalf, or open or close [the gates to either] for me. And just as little can they believe or not believe on my behalf, or force my faith or unbelief. How he believes is a matter for each individual's conscience, and this does not diminish [the authority of] secular governments. They ought therefore to content themselves with attending to their own business, and allow people to believe what they can, and what they want, and they must use no coercion in this matter against anyone.

[31] Somewhat incautiously Luther here inculpates the Emperor in person; in *Warnung an seine lieben Deutschen (Warning to his dear Germans)*, 1531, he went to some lengths to exonerate the Emperor, blaming instead the latter's counsellors.
[32] Luther is using an idiom which means: to submit to searching enquiry.

Faith is free,[33] and no one can be compelled to believe. More precisely, so far from being something secular authority ought to create and enforce, faith is something that God works in the spirit. Hence that common saying which also occurs in Augustine:[34] no one can or ought to be forced to believe anything against his will.

Those blind and wretched people do not realize what a pointless and impossible thing they are attempting. However strict their orders, and however much they rage, they cannot force people to do more than obey by word and [outward] deed; they cannot compel the heart, even if they were to tear themselves apart trying. There is truth in the saying: Thought is free. What is the effect of their trying to force people to believe in their hearts?[35] All they achieve is to force people with weak consciences to lie, to perjure themselves, saying one thing while in their hearts they believe another. And in this way [rulers] load on themselves the horrifying sins done by others, because all the lies and perjuries such [people with] weak consciences utter, when they are spoken under compulsion, fall back on the one who compels their being done. It would be much easier, although it may mean allowing their subjects to fall into error, just to let them err, rather than to force them to lie and profess [with their mouths] what they do not believe in their hearts. And it is not right to prevent one evil by doing another, even worse, one.

Do you want to know why God has ordained that the secular princes must come to grief in this horrible fashion? I'll tell you. [380:] God has given them perverse minds, and he means to make an end of them, just as he will make an end of their Spiritual Lordships. For my ungracious lords, the pope and bishops, should be [real] bishops[36] and preach the

---

33 Literally: 'a free work (or action)'; a striking example of Luther's habit of colloquial and casual expression, since the whole point of his theology is, of course, that faith is not a work or action of any kind, but an unmerited free gift.

34 The reason Luther cites Augustine in this context, apart from the latter's unrivalled authority amongst the Church Fathers as far as the Reformers were concerned, is that he was much more obviously, and notoriously, an authority for precisely the view Luther is denying: *Compelle intrare*, force them to enter [the Church].

35 Another one of Luther's telescoped reasoning. The text continues: 'when they know it be impossible'. I suppose this ought to have read: 'a thing they ought to know is impossible'.

36 The Reformers believed that there is no scriptural distinction between a bishop and a priest; at most an administrative distinction of competences, for order's sake, is tolerable. Nonetheless, the retention of bishops in the Lutheran churches seems congruent with the attitude of Luther, and was also Calvin's original stance. Note, incidentally, that even in 1523, Luther was still prepared to concede some kind of (very chastened) role to the papacy.

Word of God; but they have left off doing so and have become secular[37] princes, ruling by means of laws that concern only life and goods. They have managed to turn everything upside down: they ought to rule souls with God's Word, inwardly, and instead they rule castles, towns, countries and peoples, outwardly, and torment souls with unspeakable murders. And the secular lords, who should rule countries and peoples outwardly, do not do so either; instead, the only thing they know how to do is to poll and fleece, heap one tax on another, let loose a bear here, a wolf there. There is no good faith or honesty to be found amongst them; thieves and villains behave better than they do, and secular government is sunk as low as the government of the spiritual tyrants. God has made them to be of perverse minds and has deprived them of their senses, so that they want to rule spiritually over souls, just as the spiritual authorities want to rule in a worldly* manner. And [God's purpose in all this is] that they should thoughtlessly pile up on themselves the sins of others, earn his hatred and that of mankind, until they are ruined along with bishops, parsons and monks, all knaves together. And then they blame everything on the Gospel, blaspheming God instead of confessing their guilt, and saying that it is our preaching that has done this,[38] whereas it is their perverse wickedness that has brought it on them, and they deserved it and continue to deserve it; the Romans said just the same, when they were destroyed. And here you have God's judgement on these great men. But they do not realize it, in order that God's grave counsels may not be frustrated by their repentance.[39]

But you will reply: doesn't St Paul say in Romans 13[1]: 'Let every soul be subject to power and superiority'? And Peter, that we are to be subject to every human ordinance? [1 Pet. 2.13]? You are quite right,

---

[37] A particularly clear example of the ambiguity of Luther's term *weltlich*: although 'secular' is correct, Luther's point is plainly to stress the worldliness of papal and episcopal concerns and preoccupations. Four sentences on in this passage, I have been obliged to render the same word as 'worldly'.

[38] A set of free-floating 'this' and 'it' here makes Luther's sense opaque. I think he means that what they deserve is the destruction to which the first part of the paragraph refers. This, however, has of course not yet come about, so presumably Luther means they *will* complain about it when it does come. The reference to the Romans is to the charges they made against Christianity, which Augustine's *City of God* was in part designed to refute.

[39] Behind this passage lies the difficult doctrine that God hardens the hearts of sinners, so that they accumulate guilt and therefore deserve the eternal punishment meted out to them by him. The difficulty is that this seems to make God responsible for the wickedness he subsequently 'punishes'. See *De servo arbitrio* [*Concerning the Unfree Will*].

and this is grist to my mill. St Paul is speaking of superiors* and power*. But I have just shown that no one has power over the soul except God. St Paul cannot be speaking of obedience where there is no power [entitled to obedience]. It follows that he is not talking about faith and is not saying that worldly authority ought to have the right to command faith. What he is talking about is outward goods, about commanding and ruling on earth. And he makes clear that this is what he means when he lays down a limit to both power and obedience: 'Give to each what is due to him, tax where tax is due, customs duties where customs duties are due, honour where honour, fear where fear' [Romans 13.7]. In other words secular obedience and power extend only to taxes, duties, honour, fear, outward things. To the same effect [381:]: 'Power is not a terror to good, but to wicked works' [Romans 13.3]. He is setting a limit to power: it is not to have mastery over faith and God's Word, but over evil-doing.

St Peter means the same when he speaks of 'human ordinance'. Now, human ordinance cannot extend to heaven and the soul, but only to the earth and the outward dealings of men with one another, matters about which men can see, know, judge, pass sentence, punish and acquit.

Christ himself summarizes all this with the admirable distinction [he draws] in Matthew 22 [21]: 'Give to the Emperor the things that are the Emperor's and to God the things that are God's.'⁴⁰ If the emperor's power extended to God's kingdom and God's power, and were not something distinct and separate, there would be no point in distinguishing the two. But, as has been said, the soul is not subject to the emperor's power. He can neither teach nor guide it; he cannot kill it or bring it to life; he cannot bind or loose it, judge it or sentence it, hold it or release it. And yet he would need to [be competent to do all of these] if he were to have the power to legislate for it and issue orders to it. But as to goods and honour, here is his proper domain. For such things *are* subject to his power.

David long ago summarized all this in a short, fine saying in Psalm 113 [in fact 115.16]: 'He has given heaven to the Lord of heaven, but the earth he has given to the children of men.' In other words, as regards whatever is on earth, and belongs to the temporal, earthly kingdom*, man can have power from God. But whatever belongs to

---

⁴⁰ I have preserved Luther's translation of the Vulgate's *Caesar* as *Kaiser* (Emperor), since I think he welcomed the anachronistic implicit reference to the Holy Roman Emperor. Cp fn. 31.

heaven and to the eternal kingdom, is subject to the Lord of heaven alone. And Moses was mindful of this when he says in Genesis 1[26]: 'God said: let us create men, that shall rule over the animals and the fish in the water and the birds in the air.' All this concedes no more than outward rule to men. And in sum, what is meant is, as St Peter says in Acts 4 [in fact 5.29]: 'We must obey God rather than men.' And with this he is evidently setting a limit to secular authority. For if we were bound to do everything those with authority in the world tell us to do, there would be no point in saying 'We must obey God rather than men.'

So, if a prince or a secular lord commands you to adhere to the papacy, to believe this or that, or to surrender books, then your answer should be: it is not fitting for Lucifer to sit next to God. My good Lord, I owe you obedience with my life and goods. Command me what lies within the limits of your authority, and I will obey. But if you command me to believe, or to surrender my books, I will not obey. For then you [will have] become a tyrant and overreach[ed] yourself, commanding where you have neither right or power*.[41] If he then takes away your goods and punishes you for your disobedience, then blessed are you, and you should thank God for counting you worthy to suffer for the sake of his Word. Let the fool rage; [382:] he shall surely find his judge. But I say to you: if you do not resist him and let him take away your faith or your books, then you will truly have denied God.

Let me give you an example. In Meissen, Bavaria and the Mark, and in other places too, the tyrants have issued a decree, ordering [all] copies of the New Testament to be surrendered to their offices. What subjects [of these rulers] must do is this: they must not surrender a page, not even a letter, on pain of their soul. Whoever does so, is surrendering Christ to Herod; is a murderer of Christ, as Herod was. They should suffer their houses to be forcibly* [*mit Gewalt*] invaded and ransacked, whether it is their books or their goods that are taken. Evil is not to be resisted, but suffered. Of course, you should not approve what is done, or lift a finger or walk a single step to aid and abet them in any way, nor should you obey. These tyrants act as worldly[42] princes are meant to act. Worldly princes is what they are. But the

---

[41] Luther is here adopting the more cautious version of the scholastic doctrine concerning *ultra vires*, according to which a ruler does not cease to be a ruler for *ultra vires* acts, but is simply to be disobeyed in respect of these particular acts.

[42] In this passage, translating *weltlich* as 'secular' would lose altogether the connection with the following lines, where the connection with the 'world' (*Welt*) and 'worldliness' is explicitly made. Cf. Glossary: secular.

world is God's enemy, and therefore they must do what is at variance with God, but congenial to the world, in order to retain their honour and remain worldly princes. And so you should not be surprised at their raging and stupidity against the Gospel. They must be true to the titles they bear.

You should know that a prudent prince has been a rare bird in the world since the beginning of time, and a just prince an even rarer one. As a rule, princes are the greatest fools or the worst criminals on earth, and the worst is always to be expected, and little good hoped for, from them, especially in what regards God and the salvation of souls. For these are God's jailers and hangmen, and his divine wrath makes use of them to punish the wicked and maintain outward peace. Our God is a mighty lord, and this is why he must have such noble, well-born, rich hangmen and beadles, and will have them receive riches, honour and fear from everyone in heaped measure. It is his divine will and pleasure that we should call his hangmen 'gracious lords', fall at their feet and be subject to them in all humility, so long as they do not overreach themselves by wanting to become pastors instead of hangmen. If a prince should happen to be prudent, just or a Christian, then that is one of the great miracles and a most precious sign of divine favour on the land. But in the ordinary run of things, what Isaiah says in 3[4] holds good: 'I will give them children for princes, and gawpers shall be their lords.' And Hosea 13[11]: 'I shall give you a king in my wrath, and out of disfavour take him away again.' [383:] The world is too wicked to deserve princes much wiser and more just than this. Frogs must have storks.

But you will again object that secular authority does not compel belief; it merely, by the use of outward means, prevents people from being led astray by false doctrine. How else could heretics be restrained? The answer is: it is for bishops to do that; that task* has been assigned to them and not to rulers. The use of force* can never prevent heresy. Preventing it requires a different sort of skill; this is not a battle that can be fought with the sword. This is where God's Word must fight. And if that does not win, then secular power can certainly not succeed either, even if it were to fill the world with blood. Heresy is a spiritual thing; it cannot be struck down with steel, burnt with fire or drowned in water. God's Word alone can [conquer] here; as St Paul says in 2 Corinthians 10[4f]: 'Our weapons are not carnal ones, but are mighty in God, to destroy all the counsels and eminences that rise up against the knowledge of God, and they take captive all the senses in the service of Christ.'

And indeed neither faith nor heresy are ever stronger than when mere force[43], rather than the Word of God is used against them. For [in that case] people take it for granted that force is not being used in the cause of right, and that those who use it are acting unjustly, precisely because they are acting without God's Word and because they cannot think of any other way of furthering their aims except by mere force, like animals that have no use of reason. Even in secular matters force cannot be used unless guilt has first been established by reference to the law. And it is all the more impossible to use force without right and God's Word in such high, spiritual matters [as heresy]. What clever princes they are! They mean to drive out heresy, but cannot attack it except with something that gives it new vigour, bringing themselves under suspicion and justifying the heretics. My friend: if you want to drive out heresy, then you must first hit on a way of uprooting it from the heart, and breaking its hold on the will. And you will not do that by using force; you will merely strengthen it. What point is there in reinforcing heresy in hearts, even if you do weaken it outwardly by shutting up people's mouths or forcing them to pretend? God's Word, on the other hand, enlightens the heart and with that all heresy and error will fall away by themselves.

It is of this way of destroying heresy that the prophet Isaiah spoke when he prophesied (Isaiah 11[4]): 'He will strike the earth with the rods of his mouth, and will kill the godless with the spirit of his lips.' [384:] You can see from this that it is words that will bring about the death and conversion of the godless. In short, such princes and tyrants do not know that fighting against heresy is fighting against the devil who takes possession of hearts by means of error. As Paul says in Ephesians 6[12]: 'Our struggle is not against flesh and blood, but against spiritual evil, against the princes that rule this darkness etc.' And therefore as long as the devil is not rejected and driven out of the heart, destroying his instruments by fire and sword has as much effect on him as fighting against it with a straw would have on lightning. Job dealt with all this

---

[43] In this sentence and the three following, Luther is contrasting *Gewalt*, which is here translated as 'mere force' (although Luther also uses it to mean 'power' and 'authority' [see the Introduction, p. xv]), and *Recht*, which may mean either 'what is right', 'justice', or 'law'. Since a translator is forced to make a distinction in express words where Luther makes none, the verbal continuity of Luther's original is lost. See Glossary: law.

amply when he said (Job 41[18]): 'The devil looks on iron as mere straw and fears no power on earth.' And experience teaches the same. For even if all Jews and heretics are burnt, no one is vanquished or converted thereby, or ever will be.

But a world such as this one must have this sort of rulers; heaven forbid that anyone should ever do their duty*! Bishops must abandon the Word of God and make no attempt to rule souls with it. Instead they must command the secular princes to rule souls by the sword. The secular princes for their part must allow usury, robbery, adultery, murder and other kinds of wickedness to go unchecked, and indeed commit such things themselves, and leave it to the bishops to punish them with letters of excommunication. And in this way everything is stood on its head: souls are ruled by steel, bodies by letters. So worldly[44] princes rule spiritually, and spiritual princes rule in a worldly manner. What else is there for the devil to do in this world, except to play tricks on his subjects and masquerade as in a carnival? These, then, are our 'Christian princes', the 'defenders of the faith' and 'hammers of the Turks'. Able men, on whom we can rely! And they most certainly will achieve *something* by their admirable cleverness: they will break their necks and reduce their lands and subjects to misery and penury.

I have a piece of good advice for these misguided people. Beware of the little saying in Psalm 106 [in fact 107.40]: *Effundit contemptum super principes* [He pours out his contempt on princes]. I swear to God: if you ignore this little text, and it comes into effect against you, you are lost, even if every one of you were as mighty as the Turk; and all your snorting and raving will not help you. To a considerable extent it has happened already. There are few princes whom people do not regard as fools or criminals, and their actions bear out [that judgement]; the common man is becoming knowledgeable and a mighty plague on princes (which God calls *contemptum*) is spreading amongst the common people and the common man. My fear is that there will be no way to stop it, unless princes begin to behave like princes and to rule reasonably and cautiously. People [385:] will not put up with your tyranny and arbitrariness any longer; they cannot and they do not want to. My good lords and masters, take heed. God [himself] will not put up with it any longer. This is no longer the world it was when you hunted

---

[44] See fn 42 above.

and drove your people like game. So put aside your blasphemy and violence*; take care that you act justly and let God's Word have free passage; it will, it must and it should, and you cannot stop it. If there is heresy, then let it be overcome by God's Word; that is how it should be. But if you go about drawing the sword on every occasion, then beware of someone coming along who will tell you to put your sword away, and not in God's name either.[45]

But what if you were to say: how are Christians to be ruled outwardly, seeing that there ought to be no secular Sword amongst them? [Surely] there must be superiors* amongst Christians too? My answer is that there neither can, nor ought to be any superiors amongst Christians. Rather, each is equally subject to all the rest, as St Paul says in Romans 12[10]: 'Each is to regard the next person as his superior.' And Peter (1 Pet. 5[5]): 'Be ye all subject one to another.' And this is what Christ wants (Luke 14[10]): 'If you are invited to a wedding, take the lowest place of all.' Among Christians there is no superior except Christ alone. And how can there be superiority [or inferiority] when all are equal, and all have the same right*, power, goods and honour? No one desires to be another's superior, for everyone wants to be the inferior of the rest. How could one establish superiors amongst such people, even if one wanted to? Nature will not tolerate superiors when no one wants to be, or can be, a superior. But where there are no people of [the latter] sort, there are no true Christians either.

What of priests and bishops? Their government is not one of superiority or power, but rather a service and an office*. For they are not higher or better than other Christians.[46] And therefore they ought not to impose any laws or commands on others without their consent and permission. Their government, on the contrary, is nothing but furtherance of the Word of God, guiding Christians and overcoming heresy by means of it. As has been said, Christians can be governed by nothing except the Word of God alone. For Christians must be governed in faith, not by outward works. But faith cannot come by human words, only by God's Word. As St Paul says in Romans 10[17]: 'Faith comes by hearing, but hearing comes through the Word of God.'

---

[45] I think this is an allusion to Christ's words to Peter in the Garden of Gethsemane, Matthew 26.52; Luther is saying that it will not be Christ who tells rulers to put away their swords, but the common man.

[46] This is a reference to Luther's crucial (and highly ambiguous) doctrine of the 'priesthood of all believers', on which see the Introduction, pp. x–xi.

Those who do not have faith are not Christians and do not belong to
Christ's kingdom, but to the kingdom of the world, to be coerced and
ruled by the Sword and [386:] by external government. Christians [on
the other hand] do everything that is good, without any compulsion,
and have all they need in God's Word. But of this I have written much
and often elsewhere.

Part Three

Now that we know how far [the competence of] secular authority
extends, it is time to consider how a prince should go about exercising
it. [I am writing this] for the sake of those who want to be Christian
rulers and lords, and who give some thought to their own salvation;
there are very few of that sort. Christ himself describes the character of
secular princes when he says in Luke 22[25]: 'The secular princes rule,
and those who are superiors use force*.'47 For when they are born or
chosen as rulers, they imagine themselves entitled to be served, and to
rule by force. Now, whoever wants to be a Christian prince must
abandon any intention of lording it over people and using force. For all
life that is lived and sought after for one's own benefit is cursed and
damned: damned are all the works that do not come from love. And the
works that spring from love are those that are not done for one's own
pleasure, benefit, honour, comfort and well-being, but rather those
which are aimed wholly at the benefit, honour and well-being of others.

And hence I shall say nothing here about worldly matters and laws.
There are far too many law-books* already and the topic is [too] broad.
In any case, if a prince is not himself more prudent than those who
advise him about the law, and does not understand more than is to be
found in the texts of the law, he will surely govern as the proverb (Prov.
28[16]) says: 'A prince who lacks prudence shall oppress many with
injustice.' For however good or equitable the laws might be, they are all
subject to this exception: they cannot prevail against necessity.48
Therefore the prince must keep the laws as firmly under his own

---

47 A very strange translation, not the one that occurs in later versions of Luther's New
Testament.
48 A commonly used maxim, originally(?) from Canon Law: *Decretum Gratiani* Pt II, causa 1
qu.1, dict. ante can 39, pars VI: *Quia enim necessitas non habet legem, sed ipsa sibi facit
legem . . .*

control as he does the Sword, and use his own reason to judge when and where the law should be applied in its full rigour, and when it should be moderated. So that reason remains the ruler at all times, the supreme law and master of all the laws. In the same way, the father of a household will no doubt establish times and amounts of work and food for his servants and his children. But he must nevertheless maintain his power over these rules he has made, so that he can alter or suspend them, if it should happen that the servants are sick, or are taken prisoner, are detained, deceived or hindered in some way. [387:] He must not [for example] treat both the sick and the healthy with the same strictness. I say this so that people will not think it a precious thing, and enough by itself, to follow the written laws or the counsel of those learned in the law. More is needed.

But what is a prince to do if he is not as wise or as prudent as this, and must [therefore] allow himself to be governed by lawyers and by the letter of the law.[49] It is precisely with reference to this that I said that the prince's office* is beset by dangers, and if the prince is not wise enough to rule over both his laws and his counsellors,[50] then what will happen is what Solomon says: 'Woe to the land that has a child for its prince.' And because Solomon knew it, he despaired of all the laws, even though God [himself] had laid them down for him through [the agency of] Moses, and of all his princes and counsellors, and turned to God himself, asking him for a wise heart with which to rule the people. And a prince must follow his example: he must act in fear, and rely neither on dead books nor on living heads, but on God alone, pestering him for right understanding, greater than all books and teachers, with which to govern his subjects wisely. In short, I know nothing about what laws to recommend to a prince; I want only to instruct him how to dispose his heart with regard to whatever laws, counsels, verdicts and cases he has to deal with. If he does that, God will surely give him [the capacity] to use all laws, advice and actions to good effect.

First, then, he must look to his subjects and see to it that he is rightly disposed towards them. That is, he must direct all his efforts towards being of use and service to them. He is not to think: the land and the

---

[49] I think, but cannot establish, that this is what Luther means. His text reads 'by the lawbooks'. Cf. Glossary: law.
[50] Luther is assuming, in line with an increasingly current practice, that the counsellors of princes will be jurists.

people are mine; I shall do as I please. But rather: I belong to the people and to the land; I ought to do what is advantageous for them. I am not to see how I can lord it over them, but how they may be protected and defended, and enjoy the blessings of peace. He is to set Christ before his eyes and tell himself: here is Christ, the greatest of princes, and yet he came to serve me. He did not set about getting power, wealth and honour from me; he considered only my neediness, and used all his efforts to secure power, wealth and honour for me through him and in him. And I shall do the same. I shall not seek my own advantage at my subjects' hands, but theirs, and I will serve them in my office, protect them, listen to them, defend them, and govern only for their benefit, not for mine. A prince should therefore dispense with his might and superiority, as far as his heart and mind are concerned, and attend to the needs of his subjects as if they were his own. [388:] For this is what Christ has done for us, and these are the real works of Christian love.

To this, the reply will be: in that case, who would be a prince? The prince's office and station* would be the most wretched on earth, full of toil, trouble and discomfort. And what would happen to all the princely delights, the dancing, the hunting, racing, gaming and all the other worldly* pleasures of that sort. My rejoinder is that I am not telling secular princes how to live, but how to be Christians, to attain heaven. Everyone knows that a prince is a rare bird in heaven. Nor am I saying all this because I hold out hope that the secular princes will accept it. I say it in case there is anyone at all among them who would like to be a Christian and wants to know what he should do. But of one thing I am certain: God's Word will not be guided and twisted to suit princes; rather it is princes who are to be guided by his Word. It is enough for me if I show that it is not impossible to be both a prince and a Christian, even if it is rare and difficult. And if princes did take care that their dancing and hunting and racing did no harm to their subjects, and in other respects, too, exercised their office towards them in love, God would not be so hard as to begrudge them their dancing and hunting and racing. But such princes would soon find out that if they were to take care of their subjects as their office demands, many a dance, race and game would have to go by the board.

Second: a prince should beware of those mighty potentates, his councillors. His attitude to them should be to despise no one, but also to trust no one, at least not to the extent of leaving everything to him. For God cannot tolerate either [contempt or total trust]. He once spoke through an ass, and therefore no human being, however lowly, is to be held in contempt. But equally he let the greatest of the angels fall from heaven, and therefore no man is to be [wholly] trusted, however wise, saintly and great he might be. But all are to be heard and the prince shall wait to see through which of them God will speak and act. For the greatest evil at the courts of princes is when a prince hands over his understanding as a captive to the great men and the flatterers, and neglects to supervise things himself. If a prince is deficient here, and fools around, it is not just one person who suffers but the whole country. And therefore a prince is to place his trust in the mighty and to let them act, but in such a way as to keep the reins in his own hands. He ought not to think himself safe or allow himself to fall asleep, but should see for himself, traversing his territories on horseback (as Jehosaphat did), keeping an eye on his governors and judges. That way he will find out for himself [389:] that no one is to be trusted completely. You should not think that anyone else will take as good care of your goods and lands as you will, unless he is filled with the spirit and a good Christian. A natural man will not do it. But you do not know whether any [particular] individual is a Christian or how long he will remain one, and therefore you cannot rely on anyone completely.

You must be especially wary of those who say to you: my gracious Lord, why does Your Grace not place more trust in me than this? Who shall serve Your Grace etc.? Such a man is most certainly not pure [in his intentions] and his aim is to become master of the country and to make you his puppet. For if he were an upright and just* Christian, he would be pleased that you do not trust him, and would praise and love you for watching him closely. Godly conduct like his can and will bear your inspection, and indeed anyone's. As Christ says in John 8 [in fact 3.21]: 'Whoever does good, comes into the light so that his works may be seen, for they are wrought in God.' But the former [sort of] person is out to deceive you and to act in darkness, as Christ says [John 3.20]: 'Whoever does evil, shuns the light, that his works may not be punished.' So beware of him. And if he complains, say to him: I am guilty of no injustice towards you. God will not have me trust myself or anyone else. Reproach him for it and for making you a mere human being. [In fact, I would not put all my trust in you] even if you were an angel. Even Lucifer was not to be trusted, and therefore I shall not trust you completely either. For we should place our trust in God alone.

Let no prince imagine that his condition will be better than that of

David, the model for all princes. He had a councillor, Ahithophel by name, who was so wise that Scripture says of him that what Ahithophel declared counted as much as if God himself had been asked for counsel. And yet he sank so low that he would have betrayed and killed David, his own prince. And so David had to learn that no one at all is to be trusted. Why do you imagine God allowed such a frightful example to happen and to be recorded, unless it be to warn princes and rulers of the greatest peril and misfortune that can befall them, and to teach them to trust no one.[51] It is a wretched thing when flatterers reign at courts, and when princes rely on others and render themselves captive to them, letting them do as they please.

But you may object that if no one is to be trusted, how is any country and its people to be governed? The answer is that you do have to take the risk of entrusting people with offices, but you must not trust them or rely on them, but on God alone. [390:] You must treat those to whom you have given office as people who may fail, and so you must continue to keep watch and not allow yourself to be lulled into sleep. A coach driver trusts his horses and carriage, but he does not let them drive themselves. He keeps the reins and the whip in his own hands, and stays awake. Remember the old sayings which were learnt from experience and can be depended on: 'When the cat's away the mice will play.'[52] In other words, nothing goes right if the master does not attend to things in person and relies on advisers and servants instead. And this is as God wants it; he allows it to happen so that rulers are compelled to attend to the duties of their office themselves, just as everyone else must do their own job, and every creature must do its own work. Otherwise rulers would become fatted pigs, of no use to anyone but themselves.

Third: Let a prince take care how he meets out justice to wrong-doers. Punishing some without ruining others [who are innocent] calls for the greatest prudence and wisdom. Once again, I know of no better model than David. He once had a captain named Joab, who treacherously murdered two other captains, both just men, and so he deserved death twice over. And yet David, while he lived, did not kill him, but

---

[51] Luther's expression has come apart here and I have glossed it in my translation. It will be noted in passing that the standard claim of reformers that they adhered exclusively to the literal meaning of Scripture is pure polemic and itself must not be taken literally.

[52] Luther here offers a selection of popular saws which appear to have no English equivalent and have been omitted from the translation.

ordered his son Solomon to do it [after David's death]. This was doubtlessly because David could not do it himself without causing even more harm and upheaval. A prince must punish the wicked in such a way that in 'picking up the spoon he does not tread on the plate and break it', and does not plunge his whole country and its people into chaos for the sake of one [person's] head, and fill the land with widows and orphans. For the same reason, he must not follow those advisers and 'armchair soldiers'[53] that would push him into wars with arguments like: are we to put up with such insults and injustice? It is a very bad Christian who will put a whole country at risk for the sake of a castle. In short, the prince in such cases must act after the maxim: a person who can't wink at faults, doesn't know how to govern. So let this be his rule of conduct: where an injustice cannot be punished without a greater injustice, he should not insist on his rights*, however just his cause. He is to look to the injustices suffered by others and not the damage he suffers himself, considering what others will suffer if he exacts punishments. What have all those women and children done to deserve becoming widows and orphans, just so that you can take your revenge against a worthless mouth or a wicked hand that has done you harm?

Here you may ask: is a prince not to wage war [at all]? And are his subjects not to follow him into battle? That is a broad question, but the short answer is this. The Christian way is that no ruler is to wage war against his overlord, be he the King, the Emperor or any other liege-lord.[54] If one of these takes something, let him take it. For superiors* are not to be resisted by force, but only by witnessing to the truth.[55] If they take any notice, well and good. If not, you are guiltless and you suffer injustice for God's sake. But if your opponent is your equal or your inferior, or a foreign ruler, then you should first offer him justice and peace, as Moses taught the children of Israel. If he will not settle, then do the best you can and resist force with force, as Moses well

---

[53] Literally: iron-eaters.

[54] Luther is here assuming that power is arranged in a (in the technical sense of the term) feudal manner; in other words that everyone has a superior lord, except the supreme overlord. Those on the same rung of the ladder of super- and sub-ordination ('degree') are 'peers', and with respect to each other are as free to fight each other as the supreme lords with respect to one another.

[55] The texts here read either *Erkenntnis*, knowledge, or *Bekenntnis*, which I am adopting; both seem to me equally obscure.

describes in Deuteronomy 20[1off].[56] But here you are not to consider your own advantage, and how you can remain ruler, but your subjects, whom you owe help and protection, so that the work is done out of love. Since your whole country is placed in danger [by war], you must consider whether God will help you, so that everything does not go to wrack and ruin; and even if you cannot help making some widows and some orphans, you must at least prevent total ruin, and nothing but widows and orphans [being left].

The subjects for their part owe obedience and must set their lives and goods to it.[57] For in such a case everyone must risk his goods and even himself, for the sake of his neighbour. And in such a war, it is a Christian act, and an act of love, to kill enemies without scruple, to rob and to burn, and to do whatever damages the enemy, according to the usages of war, until he is defeated. But beware of sins and of violating women and maidens. And when the enemy is defeated, then those who surrender and submit are to be shown mercy and granted peace. In other words, act according to the maxim 'God helps the strongest.' Abraham did so when he defeated the four kings (Genesis 14[15]). Of course, he killed many and did not show much mercy until the victory was his. A case like this should be regarded as something sent by God, so that for once the land is swept clean of villains.

But what if a prince is in the wrong? Are his people obliged to obey him even then? No, because no one has a duty to act unjustly; we must obey God (who will have justice prevail), rather than men [Acts 5.29]. But what if subjects do not know whether their ruler is in the right or not? As long as they do not know and cannot find out, although they have made every effort, they may obey without danger to their souls. For in such cases, one must follow the Law of Moses in Exodus 21[13], where he writes that a murderer who has unknowingly and unintentionally killed someone shall flee to a free city and there be absolved by the courts. And whichever side is beaten, whether it be in the right or the

---

[56] The text referred to enjoins the massacring of all males and the enslavement of the women and children of a conquered population. Since I see no evidence that Luther meant deliberately to reverse the more merciful standards of conduct prevailing, I must suppose that his disposition to pretend to have learnt anything worth knowing from the Bible and not the 'sophists' or the 'whore reason' led him to cast about for a suitable text in the OT without in this case finding anything suitable. *Vim vi repellere* (to resist force with force) is of course from the Romans, not from the Bible.

[57] The sense here requires some connecting clause like: 'if a war meets all these preconditions . . .'

wrong, must take it as a punishment from God, but the side that fights and wins, in such a state of ignorance, must regard the battle as if someone fell from a roof and killed someone, and leave the matter with God. To God it is all one whether he deprives you of your goods or life by a just or an unjust lord. You are God's creature, and he may do with you as he pleases, as long as your conscience is innocent. And thus God himself excuses King Abimelech (Genesis 20[6]), when the latter took Abraham's wife. Not that the act was right, but he did not know that she was Abraham's wife.

Fourth, and this should perhaps have been the first point: as we have said above, a prince must also act like a Christian towards God. That is, he ought to subject himself to him in complete confidence and ask him for the wisdom to rule well, as Solomon did. But I have written a great deal elsewhere about faith and confidence in God and there is therefore no need to say any more now. And so we shall leave it at that and sum up. A prince ought to comfort himself in four different ways. First: towards God with real confidence and heartfelt prayer. Second: to his subjects with love and Christian service. Third: towards his counsellors and great men, with free reason and unbound understanding. Fourth: towards evil-doers with condign gravity and severity. In that way his condition* will be outwardly and inwardly right, pleasing to God and men. But he must anticipate a great deal of envy and suffering. As illustrious a man as this will soon feel the cross lying on his neck.

To end with, an addendum in reply to those who have written treatises about *restitution*,[58] that is, returning wrongfully acquired goods. This is a work for the secular Sword, about which much has been written, often with unnecessary severity. But I shall state the whole thing briefly, and eliminate all the laws and all the severity in one swoop. There is no law to be found for this, except the law of love. If you are called on to decide a case where one party ought to return something to another, and both are Christians, then the matter will soon be settled. For neither will deny the other what is his, and neither will demand it of him. But if one of them is a Christian, namely the one to whom restitution is due, then again the decision is easy. For he will

---

[58] Luther had left the word in Latin in his text, hence the explanatory clause. The topic was, and remained, a favourite with the scholastics, normally handled in commentaries on Aquinas, *Summa Theologica*, Secunda Secundae, qu. 62 and qu. 78, and it is to such discussions that Luther is here referring. It included the vexed question of borrowing or lending money at interest.

not demand its return. Equally, if it is the Christian who must return something, he will surely do so. But whether either of them is a Christian or not, this is how you ought to decide. If the debtor is poor and is unable to make restitution, whereas the other person is not poor, then you should allow free rein to the law of love and acquit the debtor. For the other party also is obliged by the law of love to remit the debt and even to give more, because of the other's need. But if the debtor is not poor, then let him make restitution, as far as he can, be it the whole, or half, or a third or quarter, as long as you leave him his house, food and clothing for himself, his wife and his children. For you would owe him these in any case, if you were able to provide them; much less should you take them away, since you do not yourself need them, and he cannot do without them.

But if both are unchristian, or if one of them will not allow matters to be judged according to the law of love, then you should leave them to find another judge, and tell the unchristian creditor that he is acting against God and natural law, even if he gets the harsh judgement in his favour [that he seeks] from a human judge. For nature teaches the same as love: I ought to do what I would have done unto me. And therefore I may not rob another, however good my claim, since I myself do not want to be robbed. What I would wish in such a case is that the other person should relinquish his right; and therefore I ought also to relinquish mine. And this is how ill-gotten gains should be treated, whether they were come by secretly or openly, so that love and natural law will always prevail. For when you judge in accordance with love, you will distinguish and decide all things easily, without law-books. But if you remove the law of love and nature, you will never hit on what is pleasing to God, even if you had swallowed all the law-books and the lawyers. On the contrary, the more you think about [what you learn from them], the more insane you become. Good judgement is not to be found in books, but from free good sense, as if there were no books. But it is love and natural law, with which all reason is filled, that confer such good judgement. From the books come oppressive and uncertain judgements. Let me give you an example.

There is a story told of Duke Charles of Burgundy. A nobleman captured his enemy. The wife of the captive came to ransom him. The nobleman said he would give the man back to her if she slept with him. The woman was virtuous, but wanted her husband released, and so she went and asked her husband whether she should do it to get him freed.

The man wanted to be free and to save his life, and permitted it. But the day after the nobleman had slept with the woman, he had her husband beheaded, and gave him back to her dead. The woman complained of this to Duke Charles who summoned the nobleman and ordered him to take the woman as his wife. After the wedding day, he had the man beheaded, placed the woman in possession of his goods and restored her honour. A truly princely punishment on wickedness.

Now no pope, no lawyer and no book could have taught him to give such a verdict. Rather it came from unfettered reason, which is greater than all the laws in books; it is so just a judgement that everyone is bound to approve it and find written in his heart that it is right. Augustine writes the same in his *De sermone Domini in monte*. And therefore written law is to be held in lower regard than reason, for indeed reason is the source of all laws, that from which they sprang. The source is not to be constricted by the stream, and reason is not to be held captive by letters.

On Civil Government

Calvin: On Civil Government
[*Institutio Christianae Religionis*, Book IV, chapter 20]

The text translated here is that of the Latin 1559 edition. However, all substantial variations from this text in any of Calvin's editions, French or Latin, have been noted either in the text itself or in the footnotes (see pp. xxvi–xxvii *above*).

Dates in square brackets signal the first appearance of the most substantial additions to the text subsequent to the first edition. [1536:] marks the return to the text of the first edition.

Square brackets indicate words inserted by the translator to complete the sense.

(FV:) indicates a minor variation from the Latin in the French versions. More significant variations are noted in the footnotes.

⟨ ⟩ indicates a portion of the Latin text omitted from the French versions.

Words followed by an asterisk are explained and discussed in the Glossary.

1.   We have established that there are two governments[1] to which mankind is subject, and we have already said enough about the first of these, which rules over the soul or the inner man, and concerns itself with eternal life. Our order of presentation now demands that we say something about the second, whose province is the establishment of a merely civil and external justice, a justice in conduct. [1559:] What I shall be discussing may seem to be quite divorced from matters of faith and spiritual doctrine[2], which are my subject. Nevertheless the course of the argument will show that I am right to link the two topics, ⟨and indeed there is no other way but to link them⟩. Especially since on the one side there are (FV: nowadays) madmen and savages bent on

---

[1] The Latin version has: a dual government (*duplex regimen*); the French, which I follow here, does not stress the connection between the two governments to the same degree.

[2] French version: from theology and doctrine about the faith,

overturning this order[3] established by God. And on the other, there are the flatterers of princes, who vaunt the might[4] of princes without [acknowledging] any bounds to it, and do not hesitate to oppose it to the overlordship of God himself. Unless we avoid both these evils, all pure faith will perish. To this should be added that it is of considerable benefit to us[5] to know what merciful care God has taken for the well-being of mankind in this respect: it should incite us to a greater zeal for his service, to show that we are not ungrateful.

[1536:] In the first place, before we go any further in this matter, we must hold fast to (FV: recall) the distinction we drew earlier. For if we do not, we will be led into a thoughtless confusion of the two things we distinguished, which are of quite different character. This often happens. For when people hear that the Gospel promises a liberty which acknowledges neither king nor magistrate* (FV: master) among men, but relies on Christ alone, they cannot imagine that any benefit can be derived from this liberty as long as they find themselves subject to any authority* whatever. And they think nothing will go well, unless the whole world is given a new face, without courts, or laws, or magistrates, or anything else of the same sort, which they imagine obstructs their freedom. But anyone who knows how to distinguish between body and soul, between this present transitory life and the eternal life to come, will not find it difficult to understand that the spiritual kingdom of Christ and civil government* are things far removed from one another. It is a Judaic folly to look for the kingdom of Christ among the things that make up this world, and to shut it up among them; our opinion, which is supported by the plainest teaching of Scripture, is that, on the contrary, the fruit we reap from grace is a spiritual fruit. We must therefore take great care to confine that liberty which is promised and offered to us in Christ within its own limits. How can the same apostle command us to stand firm and not to submit to the yoke of servitude (Gal. 5.1), and then in another place tell servants not to be solicitous about their condition, unless it is because spiritual liberty and civil servitude can stand very well together? It is in this same sense that we are to take his other sayings: 'In the kingdom of God there is neither

---

[3] French version: all polities (*polices*), even though they are established by God.

[4] The term *potentia* (might), unlike *potestas* and *imperium* (translated in this sentence as 'overlordship'), carries no connotation of legitimacy. Cf. Glossary: authority.

[5] The French version adds: in that it educates us (*pour estre edifiez*) in the fear of God.

Jew nor Greek, neither male nor female, neither slave nor free' (Gal. 3.28). And again: 'There is neither Jew nor Greek, uncircumcision or circumcision, barbarian or Scythian, ⟨slave or free⟩, but Christ is all in all' (Col. 3.11). He means that what your status or condition in the world is, and under the laws of which nation you live, are a matter of indifference, for the kingdom of Christ in no way inheres in such things.

2.   But neither does this distinction [between the two governments] in any way imply that we are to regard everything related to the polity* as something unclean, and as having nothing to do with Christians. The fantasts (FV: in our days), [1555:] who delight in unbridled licence, [1536:] rant and boast that, once we have become dead to this world through Christ, are translated to the kingdom of God and sit amongst celestial beings, it is far beneath our [new] dignity and excellence to trouble ourselves with such profane and tainted matters (FV: related to the business of this world), things quite alien to the proper concerns of a Christian. What use, they ask, are laws without trials and [law]courts? And what has a Christian to do with lawcourts? And if it is not right to kill, what use are laws and lawcourts?

We have just warned that [secular] government* and the spiritual and internal kingdom of Christ are quite distinct. But equally we must recognize that they are in no way incompatible with each other. For already, while we are still on earth, Christ's spiritual rule establishes in us some beginnings of the celestial kingdom, and in this mortal and evanescent life, allows us some foretaste of immortal and incorruptible blessedness. The end of secular government, however, while we remain in this world, is [1559:] to foster and protect the external worship of God, defend pure doctrine (FV: and religion) and the good condition of the Church, accommodate the way we live to [the requirements of] human society, [1536:] mould our conduct to civil justice, reconcile us one to another, and uphold and defend the common peace and tranquillity. I admit that all this would be superfluous if the kingdom of God as it now exists among us put an end to this present life. But if it is the will of God that during the time we are still yearning for our [true] home we are on pilgrimage[6] on earth, and that such aids are necessary for our journey, then those who deprive men of them take

---

[6] *peregrinari*; the French text drops 'pilgrimage' and substitutes 'voyage', which is, of course, also a possible reading of the Latin.

away their human nature.[7] As for their claim that the perfection of the Church of God must be so great as to make all other government and laws redundant,[8] this is stupidity, for it is to imagine a perfection which can never be found in any association of human beings. The effrontery of the wicked is so great, and their evil-doing so incorrigible, that [even] laws of great severity are scarcely enough to hold them in check. If not even force is enough to restrain them from wrong-doing, how would we expect them to act once they [were to] see that they could do what evils they pleased, with impunity?

3. But there will be a more appropriate occasion for speaking about the benefits of civil order*. For the present, the one thing that must be clearly understood is that [even] to think about abolishing it is a monstrous barbarity. Mankind derives as much benefit from it as it does from bread, water, sun and air, and its dignity is far greater than any of them. For unlike them all, civil order has not only to do with men's ⟨breathing⟩, eating, drinking and flourishing (although it certainly encompasses all these, in that it makes human association possible). Its concern, I say, is not only with these, but what is more [important], it prevents idolatries, sacrileges against the name of God, blasphemies against his truth, and other scandals to religion from emerging into the light of day and spreading (FV: being sown) among the people; it prevents disturbances of the public peace; it allows each to remain safe and unharmed in the enjoyment of what is his; it makes possible innocent contacts between people; [1539:] and it sees to the cultivation of upright conduct and decency. [1536:] In short, it upholds a public form of religion amongst Christians, and humanity amongst men. Nor ought it to worry anyone that I am now allotting to the human polity* that care for the right order of religion,[9] which I seem earlier to have placed outside [merely] human determination. I approve a political order* that makes it its business to prevent true religion, which is contained in the law of God, from being besmirched and violated with

---

[7] I have followed the French version; the Latin has *humanitas*, which was one of Calvin's favourite words but is ambiguous here.

[8] This very elliptical sentence requires completion by some such phrase as: 'any other government, apart from the uncoercive government and freely observed laws that characterize the true Church...'

[9] French version: *de bien ordonner la religion*; the Latin has: *recte constituendae religionis curam*, where *constituendae*, like all Calvin's -*stituo* compounds, is ambiguous, and might mean anything from 'setting up from new' to 'maintaining'; hence my equivocating translation. Thomas Norton's (1561) translation is: 'the care of [e]stablishing of religion...'

impunity by public and manifest sacrilege. But in doing so, I no more allow men to make laws about religion and the worship of God according to their fancy than I did before.

But if we treat the various parts of the subject separately, then the clarity of the order of exposition will itself help the reader to under-stand better what he is to think about this whole matter of civil government*. There are three such parts. The first is the magistrate*, the defender and guardian of the laws. The second is the laws them-selves, in accordance with which the magistrate governs. The third is the people, who are governed by the laws, and obey the magistrate.[10] Let us therefore first deal with the office of magistracy, and consider whether this is a legitimate vocation approved by God, what the duties of the office are, and how far its authority extends. Then, by what laws a Christian polity* must be governed. And finally, what benefit the people derive from laws and what obedience they owe to their magistrate.[11]

4. As regards the office* of magistrate: our Lord has not only declared that it is acceptable to him and approved by him, but (what is more) has particularly commended its dignity to us, by adorning it with titles of the highest honour. To cite only a few examples: all those who hold the office of magistrate[12] are called gods (Exodus 22.8; Ps. 82, 1 and 6). This title is not to be reckoned as having little importance, for it shows that they have[13] a commission from God, that they are endowed with divine authority, and that they in fact represent his person, acting in a certain sense in his place. This is not some sophism of mine;[14] rather, it is the interpretation of Christ himself when he says: 'If Scripture has called gods those to whom the Word of God is addressed...' (John 10.35). What else can this mean but that they have received a charge and commission from God to serve him in their office? And, as Moses and Jehoshaphat said to the judges they set over every city in Judah (Deut. 1.16; 2 Chron. 19.6): [they were to] execute justice not in the name of men but of God. What the wisdom of God says by the mouth of Solomon is to the same effect: it is his work that kings reign and

[10] The French version, which is in general more hortatory, has: must be governed by the laws and must obey the magistrate.
[11] French version: what use the people can make of laws, and what obedience they owe to their superior.
[12] French version: are set in positions of pre-éminence
[13] The French version of the next two lines reads: that they are authorized by him, and represent his person, being in some sense his repreentatives (*vicaires*).
[14] French version: this is not a gloss which comes from my own head;

counsellors make just decisions; that princes exercise their principate and all the judges of the earth are generous¹⁵ (Prov. 6.15 and 16). Which is as much as to say that it is not at all by the perversity of men that kings and other superiors* obtain their power over all things on earth; on the contrary it comes about by the providence and sacred ordinance of God, whose pleasure it is to have mankind governed in this manner. [1539:] ⟨For he is present with them, and indeed presides over them, when they make laws and pronounce equitable judgements⟩. [1536:] This is also clearly what Paul teaches when he numbers 'positions of authority'* amongst the gifts of God which, as they are diversely distributed to men according to the diversity of grace, so they must be used by Christ's servants for building up the Church (Rom. 12.8). [1539:] It is true that he is here referring specifically to the council of grave men¹⁶ which was established in the early Church to supervise public discipline, an office which he terms ⟨*kyberneseis*⟩ 'government' in the Epistle to the Corinthians (1 Cor. 12.28). However, since we see civil authority tending to the same end, there is no doubt that he is commending all just authority*. [1536:] And the point is made even more clearly when Paul addresses precisely this subject. For he teaches that all power* exists by divine ordinance and that there is none which is not established by God. [He goes on to say] that princes are ministers of God to honour those who act rightly and to execute the vengeance of his wrath upon evil-doers (Rom. 13.14). In this connection, we may also cite the example of holy men, some of whom ruled as kings, like David, Josiah and Hezekiah, others held high offices of state, like Joseph and Daniel, yet others had the government of a free people, like Moses, Joshua and the Judges; we know that the offices* of all of them were acceptable to God, for he declared them to be so. Hence there can be no doubt that in the sight of God civil authority (FV: superiority) is not merely a holy and legitimate vocation, but by far the most sacred and honourable of all human vocations.¹⁷

¹⁵ French version: and that the judges of the earth are equitable. The Latin could also be translated as: kings, and all the generous judges of the earth, exercise their principate.
¹⁶ In the French version Calvin uses the term 'Assembly of Elders'. He is here finding, as it were in passing, scriptural warrant for the Consistory, which was his most notable contribution to the Genevan public order.
¹⁷ Literally: in the whole life of mortal men. Is Calvin here saying that the ecclesiastical ministry is less honourable than the civil magistracy as a vocation, or is his meaning that the former is not a vocation 'in the whole life of mortal men'? The French version short-circuits the obscurity and simply reads: amongst all the other vocations.

5. [1559:] Those who want to introduce anarchy[18] reply that although there were formerly kings and judges (FV: governors) over (FV: the Jews, for they were) a rude and savage people, such a servile manner of government is wholly inappropriate nowadays; it cannot square with the perfection which Christ has brought us in his Gospel. In this they disclose their stupidity as well as their devilish pride, laying claim to a degree of perfection of which we do not see even a hundredth part in them. But, leaving aside their morals and conduct, their contention is easy enough to refute. For when David exhorts kings and all rulers (FV: princes) to kiss the Son of God (FV: as a sign of homage), he does not command them to lay down their power (FV: quit their station) and retire into private life (FV: become private persons), but rather to subject the power vested in them to Christ, so that he alone may have pre-eminence over all. In the same way Isaiah, when he promised that kings would be nursing-fathers of the Church and queens nursing-mothers (Isa. 49.23), does not strip kings and queens of their honour; on the contrary he invests them with the honourable title of protectors of the faithful servants of God.[19] For this prophecy refers to the coming of Christ. I deliberately omit many other testimonies to be found in various places [in Scripture], especially in the Psalms, which assert the right of all superiors*. But there is one place in Paul more notable than all the rest. He admonishes Timothy to have public prayers said for kings, and he at once adds the reason: so that we might live peacefully under them, in all godliness* and decency (1 Tim. 2.2).[20] With these words, he is committing the well-being of the Church to them, as its custodians and guardians.

6. [1536:] Magistrates ought to ponder this constantly, for it can be a spur to prick them to do their duty, and can bring them marvellous consolation, alleviating the difficulties (FV: and vexations) inherent in their office, which are certainly many and grave. Will they not set themselves the highest standards of integrity, prudence, clemency, moderation and innocence, when they recognize themselves to have been ordained ministers of divine justice? How will they have the effrontery to admit any iniquity to their [judgement-]seat, when they hear that it is the throne of the living God? To pronounce unjust

---

[18] French version: those who want human beings to live pell-mell, like rats in straw
[19] My translation here follows the French version.
[20] The French version reads: in the fear of the Lord and decency (*honnêtété*).

sentence with the mouth they know to be destined to be an organ of God's truth? Will their consciences allow them to sign some evil ordinance with the hand which they know to be ordained for writing God's laws? In sum, if they remember that they are representatives[21] of God, they will have to apply all their energy, zeal and solicitude to the work of representing before men an image, so to say, of the providence, protection, goodness, benevolence and justice of God. Furthermore, they must always keep in mind that if all those are accursed who do the work of executing God's vengeance deceitfully (Jer. 48.10), then all the more are they accursed, if they behave disloyally in so just a vocation. Thus, when it was Moses's and Jehoshaphat's purpose to exhort their Judges to do their duty, they could find nothing better fitted to stir their hearts than [the exhortation] we mentioned earlier: 'Be careful in what you do, for it is by no means in the name of mortal men that you execute justice, but in the name of God, who is beside you when you deliver judgement. May the fear of God therefore be upon you; and see that you act as is fitting, for there is no perversity with the Lord our God' (Deut. 1.16; 2 Chron. 19.6). And in another place it is written that 'God has stood in the assembly of the gods and that in the midst of the gods he renders judgement' (Ps. 82.1). It ought to spur them on to do their duty to hear that they are God's legates[22] and will one day have to render him an account of how they have governed their provinces. And this warning ought to carry great weight with them. For if they are guilty of some dereliction of duty, they not only wrong[23] the people by the crimes they commit against them, but God [himself], whose sacred judgements they defile. On the other hand [magistrates] may derive the amplest consolation from reflecting that theirs is not some profane occupation (FV: vocation) alien to servants of God, but a most sacred commission, for it is as God's legates that they act.[24]

7. As for those who remain unmoved by so much evidence from

---

[21] Here *vicarios, vicaires*. Cf. fns. 22 and 24 for other terms.

[22] French version: 'It ought to touch the hearts of all [superiors]...' A legate was an emperor's (and also of course a pope's) plenipotentiary envoy. The French version, evidently regarding the point as too technical, has 'representatives' (*lieutenants*) and commission (*charge*).

[23] *iniuria, iniure*: ambiguous as between 'harm' and 'injustice'.

[24] *legatione funguntur*; the French version again omits the 'legate' allusion (cf. fn. 22 above) and simply says *office*.

Scripture and who dare to condemn this holy ministry (FV: vocation)[25] as something entirely contrary to Christian religion and godliness*: is this not to insult God himself? It is impossible to despise God's ministers without dishonouring God himself. But in fact it is not magistrates that such people reject, but rather God himself and his rule. For if it was rightly said about the people of Israel when they rejected Samuel's rule (1 Sam. 8.7), that they would not allow [God] to reign over them, why might the same thing not equally well be said today about those who allow themselves licence to malign all positions of authority* instituted by God? But [they claim that] the Lord forbids all Christians to meddle with kingdoms and positions of authority, for he tells his disciples that the kings of the nations lord it over them, but that it is not to be so among [Christians], where he who is first should become the least (Luke 22.25 and 26). What skilful interpreters! A dispute had arisen between the disciples (FV: apostles) about which one of them ought to be accorded pre-eminence. To rebuke such vanity, the Lord declares that their ministry is not like kingship, where one has precedence over all the rest. In what way, may I ask, does this comparison diminish the dignity of kings? In fact, does it prove anything at all, except that the office (FV: estate) of king is not the [same thing as] the ministry of an apostle? What is more, although there are various sorts and types of magistracy (FV: superiors), they nevertheless do not differ at all in one respect, namely that we are to accept them as orders[26] established by God. Paul includes them all when he says that there is no power but from God (Rom. 13.1). And the form which was least palatable to men has been singled out for commendation above all the rest, namely power exercised by one man. [This] was never acceptable to the heroic and nobler spirits in the old days,[27] because this [form of rule] carries with it the common servitude of all except the one person, to whose will and pleasure all the rest are subjected. But Scripture, to obviate the malignity of such opinions,[28] affirms specifi-

---

[25] Calvin here and in the next sentence uses the same words *ministerium/ministère* and *minister/ministre* by which he elsewhere denotes pastors and their office. The implicit comparison is quite deliberate, for he uses the description repeatedly; cf. fns. 55, 77, 80, 82, 90 below for other instances.

[26] French version: as ministers ordained by God. The Latin term is *ordo*, meaning a rank, status, estate, station. Cf. Glossary: Luther – estate.

[27] French version: has never been congenial to any persons of excellent and noble spirit,

[28] French version: this malignity of [merely] human judgements

cally that it is by the providence of the divine wisdom that kings reign (Prov. 8.15), and particularly commands that kings be honoured (1 Pet. 2.17).

8.²⁹   It would be [1536: It is] utterly pointless for private men, who have no right to decide how any commonwealth* whatever is to be ordered, to debate what would be the best state of the commonwealth [1543:] in the place where they live.³⁰ [1536:] Besides, it would be rash to [try to] settle the matter without [making] qualifications, seeing that what is crucial to this discussion is circumstances. And even if one compares various forms of government* without taking circumstances into account, it is not easy to decide which is the most beneficial [form], so evenly balanced are their respective advantages and disadvantages. Kingship is liable to collapse into tyranny. But aristocracy turns into faction almost as easily. And [the decline from] popular rule into sedition is the easiest of all. [1543:] I readily admit that if the three forms of government which philosophers refer to are considered in themselves, then aristocracy, either pure or a mixed form compounded of aristocracy and polity,³¹ greatly excels all the others. [1559:] This however is not because that form is inherently better, but [rather] because it is very rare for kings to exercise such self-control that their will never differs from what is equitable and right. And it is equally rare

²⁹ This is the most, and most repeatedly, altered section in the whole chapter and also the one where the French and Latin versions, as well as the successive editions in each version, differ most widely. I have therefore offered a separate translation of the French version in an addendum (p. 84). A discussion of the significance of the successive additions (there were no subtractions) may be found in my *Christian Polity* (Cambridge: Cambridge University Press, 1982), pp. 153-5.

³⁰ The original text of 1536 seemed to debar everyone except 'public persons', i.e. rulers, from even abstract discussion of the question of the best form of government/polity. Since this was a staple topic of discussion amongst scholastics and humanists alike, and since in any case by 1543 Calvin too (in the relevant sense a 'private person' himself) meant to discuss the subject, he added 'in the place where they live'. Note too that the Latin is ambiguous enough to allow the reading: 'private men, who have no right to discuss (*deliberare*) any matter of public business.' I am not sure that this is not what Calvin meant; at any rate, his casual or equivocal expression is symptomatic of his hostility to political enterprises of any kind on the part of private men.

³¹ Calvin is here using the Aristotelian term *politeia* in its Latin version. Aristotle in his *Politics*, Bk 4, ch. 2, distinguished between two forms of citizen rule, a corrupt form which he called 'democracy' and an uncorrupt one, a species of legal or 'constitutional' government, which he called 'polity'. Scholastic writers did not always trouble to make this distinction, and usually used the term 'democracy' indiscriminately for all forms of popular government. It will be noticed that Calvin himself follows this practice in the French version. See Glossary: polity.

56

for kings to be equipped with such prudence and acuity of understanding as to be able [always] to discern what is good and useful. It is therefore the vices or defects of mankind that make it safer and more tolerable that several persons should govern [jointly], all of them assisting, instructing and admonishing one another; so that if one of them arrogates more to himself than he is entitled to do, there will be others to act as his censors and masters, to curb his licence. [1543:] Experience has always borne this[32] out, and the Lord confirmed it by his own authority when he instituted an aristocracy bordering on a polity[33] among the Israelites, since he wished to keep them in the best possible condition [1559:] until such time as he would bring forth an image of Christ in [King] David. [1543:] I freely admit that no form of government is better than that in which liberty and the right degree of restraint are reconciled, [a government] rightly ordered so as to be durable. Accordingly, I regard those as most fortunate[34] who are allowed to enjoy such a condition; and if they always do their utmost to preserve and maintain it, I admit that this is to do no more than their duty. And what is more, the magistrates[35] [under this form of government] ought to make every effort to prevent any diminution, still less violation, of that liberty of which they have been appointed guardians. If they are slothful or unconcerned in the matter, they are traitors to their office and their country.

But if those whom the Lord has assigned some other form of government were to treat what I have said as having any relevance to themselves, and consequently were to be tempted to bring about some upheaval or change, it would not merely be a foolish and pointless idea, but a pernicious one as well. [1536:] If you do not confine your reflections to just a single commonwealth, but consider either the world as a whole, or at least some regions farther afield, you will find that it was not without a good purpose that divine providence has so disposed that different regions are governed by different sorts of

---

[32] A free-floating 'it' here seems to mean 'the truth of what I am arguing'.
[33] See note 31 above.
[34] The word Calvin uses is *beatos*, 'blessed', which I cannot bring myself to use; 'happy' would be equally bad. Of course, Calvin rejected any notion of 'fortune', so my own rendition is not entirely satisfactory either, but Calvin himself occasionally uses the term, e.g. in s. 28.
[35] Calvin is here, as usual, using the republican term for a holder of public office (cf. Glossary: magistrate), but no other word would have been appropriate in this specific context.

regime*. For just as elements only cohere because they are differently proportioned, so [each polity] is most firmly held together only in virtue of a certain inequality. But all this is superfluous for those for whom the will of God is reason enough. For if it has seemed good to him to set kings above kingdoms and senators or other officials[36] over free commonwealths*, then we for our part must be obedient and dutiful to whomever he has appointed ruler over the place we inhabit.

9.   This is the place to say a word in passing about the duties of magistrates*, about what they are and what the Word of God says of them. [1559:] And even if Scripture did not teach us that the magistrate's competence extends to both Tables of the Decalogue,[37] we could still learn it from the pagan writers.[38] For there is not one of them who, when dealing with the duties of magistrates, law-making and the civil order,[39] did not begin with religion and divine worship. By so doing, they all acknowledged that no polity can be well constituted, unless it makes duties* [owed] to God its first concern, and that for laws to attend [only] to the well-being of men, while disregarding what is owed to God, is an absurdity.[40] And so, since all philosophers give pride of place to religion, and since the whole human race has always been of one accord in respecting this [primacy], Christian princes and magistrates should be ashamed of any negligence in the performance of this duty. We have already shown that God has made what relates to religion their special business, and it is only right that they should preserve and assert his honour, whose representatives they are and by whose grace and favour they rule. Certain holy kings are much praised in Scripture for restoring the worship of God when it had been corrupted or overturned, and for making it their chief concern that religion should flourish pure and unimpaired under their rule. By contrast, the sacred history ranks anarchical conditions amongst the evils: since there was no king in Israel, each man did whatever he

---

[36] Literally 'decurions'; I do not know why Calvin chose to refer to these relatively obscure officials of the Roman Republic; the reference is dropped in the French version.

[37] It was a commonplace of theology and piety to divide the Decalogue into two Tables, the former dealing with duties to God, the latter with duties to our neighbour.

[38] In other words, from the Humanists' favourite classical authors. The emphasis on these writers being 'pagans' (my rendering of *profanis*) is dismissive, but Calvin cannot forbear to cite them all the same, when it suits his book.

[39] The French version has 'ordering the polity', the Latin simply, 'condition of the polity (*publico statu*)'.

[40] French version: is to put the cart before the horse (literally: oxen).

pleased (Judg. 21.25).[41] Hence those who would confine their efforts solely to doing justice amongst men, without any concern for God, stand convicted of stupidity.[42] As if God had established superiors in his name to decide worldly controversies, but had omitted to provide for what is of far greater moment, namely that he should be worshipped purely, according to the rule laid down in his Law. But such is their passion for innovating in everything with impunity, that these turbulent (FV: spirits) want the elimination of everyone who would defend godliness* when it has been violated.

As regards the Second Table, [1536:] Jeremiah tells kings (22.3) that they should render judgement and justice, and deliver the oppressed from the hands of their detractors, neither aggrieving strangers, widows and orphans, nor doing any injustice or shedding innocent blood. To the same effect is the exhortation which we find in Psalm 82 [3, 4], that they should do justice to the poor and needy, relieve those in poverty and want, and snatch the poor and needy from the hand of their oppressor. And Moses (Deut. 1.16) tells the rulers he had appointed to govern as his representatives that they should hear the cause of their brothers, judging between brother and brother, and strangers; that they should be no respecters of persons in their judgements, hearing both the great and the small and fearing no man, because theirs is the judgement of God. I leave aside [what is written elsewhere], that kings should not accumulate horses unto themselves (Deut. 17.16), nor give their minds over to greed, nor rise up in pride over their brothers; that they should be assiduous in meditating upon the Law of God all the days of their life; that judges should be impartial (16.19); that they should accept no 'presents'; and whatever else of the same sort is to be found in Scripture. For in explaining the duty of magistrates, my purpose is not so much to teach magistrates themselves, as rather to teach others what magistrates are and why God has established them. We see, therefore, that they have been appointed protectors and vindicators of public innocence, propriety, decency and tranquillity and

[41] The French version improves on this incomplete sentence by rendering it: sacred history [counts as one] amongst the evils which the lack of a good governor brings, the fact that superstitions ran riot, for there was no king...
[42] This seems to be an allusion to Sébastien Châteillon (Castellio) and other partisans of religious toleration, with whom Calvin and his chief collaborator Theodore de Bèze had at this time much difficulty. Cf. Sébastien Châteillon (Castellio), *Conseil à la France desolée*, and the Introduction, pp. xi, xxiv; and Theodore de Bèze (Beza), *De justa haereticorum ... punitione*, and cf. Chronology pp. xxx, xxxi.

that their one endeavour must be to provide for the common peace and well-being. David declared that, once raised to the royal throne, he would show forth these virtues (Ps. 101); that is, that he would not be party to any crimes, but would hate the unrighteous, the calumniators and the proud, and would search everywhere for upright and faithful counsellors (Ps. 101). But since magistrates cannot carry out [their appointed task] unless they protect good men from the injustices of the wicked, and help and protect the oppressed, they have been armed with power*, to repress ⟨evil-doers and⟩ malefactors, whose wickedness disturbs and troubles the public peace. We know by experience the truth of Solon's saying that all commonwealths* are kept in being by rewards and punishments; take these away and all the discipline of polities* collapses and vanishes. For in many hearts a concern for what is right and just grows cold unless honours are assigned to virtue; and the depravity of the wicked cannot be checked except by severity and the knowledge that they will be punished. And these two [rewards and punishments] are included in what the prophet says (Jer. 21.12 and 22.3) when he commands kings and other superiors to render judgement and justice. For justice means placing the innocent under one's protection, cherishing them, safeguarding them, defending and delivering them. And judgement means taking a stand against the effrontery of the wicked, repressing their violence and punishing their crimes.[43]

10. But here, it seems, a difficult and vexing question arises: if the Law of God (Exod. 20.13; Deut. 5.17; Matt. 5.21) forbids all Christians to kill, and if the prophet (Isa. 11.9 and 65.25) foretells that they shall neither afflict nor harm anyone on God's holy mountain (in other words the Church), then how can magistrates be dutiful* to God and shed blood at the same time? But if we understand that when magistrates inflict punishments, it is not any act of their own, but only the execution of God's [own] judgements, we will not be inhibited by any scruple on this score. The Law of God prohibits killing. But in order that murders shall not go unpunished, the Lawgiver himself puts the sword into the hands of his ministers, to be used against all murderers. Afflicting and harming are not the actions of godly* men, but to avenge, at God's command the afflictions of the godly is not 'afflicting or

---

[43] This highly contrived exegesis of what Calvin must surely have known is merely an emphatic pleonasm of the kind habitual in the OT illustrates Calvin's reluctance to allow any independent authority to merely human reason, as opposed to Scripture.

harming'. If only this consideration were always present in our minds: in punishing, nothing is done by human presumptuousness but by God's command and authority. ⟨And when that comes first, there is never any straying from the right path.⟩ [44] Unless perhaps divine justice is to be bridled, so as to prevent it punishing crimes. [45] And if it is not permissible to impose a law on God, why do we slander his ministers? [46] They do not bear the sword in vain, says St Paul (Rom. 13.4), for they are God's ministers to execute his wrath and wreak vengeance on evil-doers. Therefore, if princes and other superiors know that there is nothing more acceptable to the Lord than their obedience, let them spare no effort in exercising this ministry, if indeed they have any desire to please God by their piety*, obedience and justice. Certainly it was this desire that impelled Moses when he slew the Egyptian, knowing himself to be destined by the power of God to be the liberator of his people (Exod. 2.12); and again when he slew three thousand in one day, to punish the idolatry of the people (32.27). And it was the same desire that moved David, when at the end of his life he commanded his son Solomon to kill Joab and Shimei (1 Kings 2.5). This too is why he mentions (Ps. 101.8) 'destroying the wicked of the earth' amongst the royal virtues, so that all who work iniquity might be eliminated from the city of God. Here also belongs the praise which is accorded to Solomon (Ps. 45.7): 'You have loved justice and hated iniquity.' How could Moses, normally of a gentle and peaceable disposition, reach such a pitch of cruelty as to run through the camp eager for further slaughter, when he was already bespattered and dripping with the blood of his brothers? How was it that David, all his life a man of great gentleness, made this bloodthirsty last will and testament with his dying breath: that his son should not allow Joab and Shimei to go grey-haired and in peace to their graves (1 Kings 2.3; 6.8)? The savagery (FV: if indeed it should be called that) of both Moses and David sanctified those hands which they would have sullied by mercy, for it was the vengeance which

---

[44] All the French versions here add the following: hence it is easy to conclude that in this respect, they [the magistrates] are not subject to the general law, by which the Lord does indeed bind the hands of all mankind, but places no fetters on his own justice, which he executes by the hands of magistrates. In the same way, when a prince forbids all his subjects to carry weapons or to wound anyone, he nevertheless does not [thereby] prevent his own officers from executing that justice which he has specifically committed to them.

[45] French version: when we take that into consideration, we shall find nothing to reproach in public vengeance, unless we propose to impede God's justice in the punishment of malefactors.

[46] See fn. 25 above.

God had committed to them that they were carrying out. 'It is an abomination in kings to do iniquity', says Solomon (Prov. 16.12), 'for the throne is made lasting by justice.' And again (20.8): 'The king who sits in the throne of judgement casts his eye over all malefactors' (FV: that is, to punish them). Again (20.26): 'A wise king scatters the unrighteous* and turns [i.e. breaks] them on the wheel'; and (25.4 and 5): 'separate the dross from the silver, and a vessel shall come forth to the man who makes the cast; remove the unrighteous from the king's sight, and his throne shall be established in righteousness'. And again (17.15): 'To acquit the unrighteous and condemn the righteous are both abominations unto the Lord.' And (17.11): 'The rebellious man draws down calamity upon himself and a cruel messenger is sent to him'. (24.24): 'Whosoever says to an unrighteous man, you are just, him the people and the nations shall vilify.' The true justice [of rulers], then, is to pursue the evil-doers and the unrighteous with drawn sword. If [rulers] sheath their sword and keep their hands unsullied by blood, while the wicked roam about massacring and slaughtering, then so far from reaping praise for their goodness and justice, they make themselves guilty of the greatest possible injustice. But let there be no peremptory or savage harshness, nor the sort of court which has been rightly called 'the rock on which accused men founder'.[47] For I am not one of those who favour an insatiable savagery, nor do I think an equitable verdict can be pronounced unless clemency is always in attendance, that 'best counsellor and most certain preserver of royal thrones', as Solomon says (Prov. 20.28). Someone[48] once rightly called it the chief virtue of princes. The magistrate must however exercise care neither to damage more than he mends, by excessive severity, nor to lapse into a most cruel 'humanity', allowing himself to be ennervated by a superstitious attachment to clemency into a soft and dissolute indulgence, to the destruction of many. For it was pointedly remarked by someone ⟨when Nerva was emperor⟩, that it is bad to live under a prince who permits nothing, but much worse to live under one who permits everything.

11.   From time to time it is necessary for kings and peoples to take up arms in order to carry out this kind of public vengeance. And our previous argument also allows us to conclude that wars engaged in for

---

[47] The French version replaces the classical allusion to the tribunal of Cassius by: or that a judge should be like a gibbet already prepared.

[48] Seneca, a commentary on whose *On Clemency* was Calvin's first published work.

this purpose are legitimate. For if kings and peoples have conferred on them the power* to preserve the tranquillity of their territories, to repress the seditious upheavals fomented by rebellious men, to help those oppressed by violence and to take measures against the wicked, what better occasion can there be for employing that power, than in order to quell the fury of someone who disturbs the peace and quiet not only of private individuals but of entire communities? Someone who foments sedition and perpetrates violence and oppression and other outrages? If it is the duty [of kings and peoples] to act as guardians and champions of the laws, they must also make every effort to frustrate the enterprises of those whose crimes undermine the discipline of laws. Besides, if they are right to punish criminals by whose misdeeds only a few are harmed, are they to let criminality that afflicts and lays waste an entire region go scot-free? It is of no consequence here whether it is a king or the lowest of the mob who invades a foreign region where he has no jurisdiction, to murder and pillage;[49] all of them are equally to be regarded as criminals and punished accordingly. [1543:] Natural justice and their office equally demand that princes must be armed (FV: use the sword) not only to repress private wrong-doing by means of judicial penalties, but also to defend, by means of war, the territories committed in trust to them when they are invaded by enemies. And wars of this sort the Holy Spirit declares to be legitimate by the testimony of many places in Scripture.

12. If someone here objects that there is no proof-text or example in the New Testament which shows that war is permissible for Christians, my reply is this: in the first place, the reasons for waging war which existed formerly, still exist today.[50] Conversely, there is nothing which prevents a magistrate from defending his subjects. Furthermore, we are not to seek an explicit discussion of matters of this sort in the apostolic writings (FV: doctrine); their purpose is to teach the spiritual kingdom of Christ, not to shape[51] a polity. In any case, Scripture does indeed offer evidence in passing that Christ by his coming changed nothing in this regard. For if Christian teaching[52] (to use Augustine's term) condemned all wars, the soldiers who sought advice about

---

[49] This phrase is from the French version; the Latin has the limp and untranslatable *eam hostiliter vexat*.

[50] A telescoped text, made even more opaque in the French, which (I think) requires completion by some clause such as 'and which were valid then, are still valid now'.

[51] *Formare*; the French version is: to order (or set up, *ordonner*) earthly polities.

[52] *disciplina*, which also means discipline.

salvation would have been told to throw away their weapons and to quit the army at once. What they were in fact told, however, was: 'Strike no one, do injustice to no one, and be content with your pay' (Luke 3.14). If Christ commanded them to be content with the pay of soldiers, he was [evidently] not forbidding them to fight as soldiers. [1536:] But all magistrates are to take the greatest care not to give in, however little, to their passions; rather, if penalties are to be inflicted, they are not to allow themselves to be carried away by anger, or hatred, or implacable severity, but to have compassion on our common [human] nature, as Augustine says, even in those whose crimes they punish. And even though arms must indeed [sometimes] be taken up against an enemy, that is, an armed criminal, [magistrates] are not to snatch at every casual opportunity: even if an occasion presents itself, they should not avail themselves of it unless compelled by a necessity which permits no escape. For much more is demanded of Christians than was demanded by the pagan[53] who wanted war to be a sort of searching for peace; everything else ought to be tried first before the recourse to arms. And in both kinds of activity [war and punishing criminals], magistrates must not allow themselves to be carried away by any private passion, but must be guided by a concern for the public good[54] alone. To do anything else is the worst abuse of their authority, which is given to them for the benefit and service[55] of others, and not for their own. On this same right to wage war also hinges the legitimacy of garrisons, alliances and other military provisions. I call 'garrisons' the disposition of soldiers in various cities to protect the borders of a region; 'alliances', those [treaties] which are made by neighbouring princes for mutual assistance against disturbances in their territories, and in order to join forces for the suppression of the common enemies of the human race; and 'military provisions' whatever is used in the art of war.[56]

13. Let me add this last point. Taxes of various kinds are the legitimate revenue of princes. They should employ them in the main to defray the public expenses they incur by virtue of their office, but they may also use them to maintain the splendour of their households, a thing linked in a certain way to the dignity of the high office* they bear.

---

[53] Cicero, *De officiis*, I.23.
[54] The Latin is: *publico sensu*; the French: *une courage publique*.
[55] *Ministerium*: see fn. 25 above.
[56] I am unable to say why Calvin regarded the terminology he was using as requiring glosses in both Latin and French versions.

Thus we see that David, Hezechiah, Josiah, Jehoshaphat and other holy kings, and equally Joseph and Daniel, in respect of the public person they bore, lived sumptuously from the public purse, without offending against their duties* to God in any way. And we read in Ezekiel (48.21) that a most generous tract of land was assigned to kings. [1539:] And although Ezekiel is here depicting the spiritual kingdom of Christ, nevertheless he draws his image or analogy from what is legitimate in earthly kingdoms. [1536:] But again, princes for their part are reminded [by Ezekiel] that the public revenues (FV: domains) are not their private coffers but rather the treasury of the whole people – as Paul tells us (Rom. 13.6) – which they cannot waste or squander without flagrant injustice. This is in fact almost the very life-blood of the people, which it would be the cruellest inhumanity not to use sparingly. As for their imposts, duties, and other sorts of taxes,[57] these they are to regard as assistance rendered them for the sake of public necessity alone;[58] and it would be tyrannical rapacity to vex the poor people with them needlessly. What I say here does not encourage princes to engage in costly extravagance and luxury; there is no need to fan the flames of their desires, which burn brightly enough already without any help from me. But princes must be taught what is permissible for them, since it is of the utmost importance that they should not fall into contempt of God by an impious over-confidence,[59] and that whatever it is they undertake, they should undertake it only when they have a pure conscience before God. And it is not irrelevant that private persons too should be taught about this, so that they do not allow themselves a ⟨rash and thoughtless⟩ reviling of princes for their expenditures, even if these do exceed the ordinary and civil[60] measure.

14.   Next in order ⟨in the polity⟩, after magistrates, come the laws, those strongest sinews of the commonwealth or, as Cicero, following

---

[57] In both the Latin and the French versions, Calvin uses various specialized synonyms for 'taxes', which I have not attempted to translate precisely, any more than the French precisely translates the Latin. He seems, however, to distinguish between permanent revenues from the royal domains, and more *ad hoc* taxes; cf. next note.

[58] A reference, I take it, to the maxim beloved of tax-payers until well into the modern period, that 'the king should live of his own', and that taxes are either *ad hoc* provisions for a state of emergency, or concessions entitling to a *quid pro quo*.

[59] Elsewhere Calvin distinguishes between *confidentia* (presumptuousness, self-reliance) which is characteristic of the reprobate, and a well-grounded assurance (*fiducia*), typical of the elect.

[60] The French merely reads: 'the usual order and measure'; the Latin *civilis*, citizen-like, is for the later Calvin a term of approval; it might be rendered as 'modest'.

Plato, calls them, the soul without which magistracy cannot survive, just as the laws in their turn are quite powerless without the magistrate. And thus nothing could be more true than the saying that the law is a silent magistrate and the magistrate a living law.[61] But although I have undertaken to say what laws are to establish[62] a Christian polity*, there is no reason in that for anyone to expect from me a long disquisition about which laws would be best; that is an interminable topic and not relevant to my subject. I shall merely, as it were in passing, note a few things about what laws [such a polity] can justly employ and by which it can be rightly governed, in the sight of both God and men. And I would have preferred to pass over even this in silence, but for the fact that I see many falling into dangerous errors on this score. For there are some[63] who deny that any commonwealth* can be properly ordered if it is governed simply by the laws common to all nations, but without embracing the political laws of Moses. Others may concern themselves, if they wish, with how dangerous and seditious this opinion is; for my purposes it is enough to show that it is a false and stupid one. We must bear in mind here the commonplace[64] division of the whole Law of God, as promulgated by Moses, into moral, ceremonial and judicial parts, and we must consider these parts separately, so as to be certain which of them apply [directly] to us, and which less so.[65] Nor should we allow ourselves to be detained by the quibble that judicial and ceremonial laws also have to do with morality. The old authors who handed down[66] this division knew well enough that ceremonial and judicial laws have a bearing on morality, but did not call them 'moral' laws, because they could be changed and abrogated without danger to morals. They reserved the term 'moral' for that part of the Law on which the true holiness of morals ⟨and the immutable rule of right living⟩ depends.

---

[61] A favourite saw of the time, originally (it seems) from Cicero.

[62] *consistere*; literally: by what laws a Christian polity is to stand [or exist]. The French version says *doit estre gouvernée*.

[63] The difficulty Calvin here confronts is of the Reformation's own making, and arises from its fundamentalist hostility to 'merely human traditions', laws and customs.

[64] Calvin apparently cannot bring himself to acknowledge that it is an opinion of the despised scholastics that he is here invoking. Nevertheless that is what it is; e.g. Aquinas, *Summa Theologica*, Ia IIae, ss. 94ff. Somewhat later in this section he again equivocates, attributing this opinion to the 'old authors' (*veteres/anciens*).

[65] Calvin is here reluctant to say that some parts do not apply at all, although that is what his sense requires. But the French is explicit.

[66] French version: found [out?]

15.   To begin then with the moral law. It has two headings, under the former of which we are commanded to worship God in pure faith and godliness*, under the latter to love our fellow man with unfeigned love. This is the true and eternal rule of justice, laid down for all those in every age and of every nation who want to order their lives in accordance with the will of God. It is his eternal and immutable will that he be worshipped by all of us and that we should truly love one another. The ceremonial law was a way of educating[67] the Jews; this is how it seemed good to the Lord to train them while they were in their infancy (so to speak), until that time of fulness when he would manifest the totality of his wisdom to the earth, and show forth the truth of those things which he had formerly represented only obscurely and in figures. In the judicial laws which he gave the Jews to serve them as their civil order*, he set down certain rules of justice and equity by which they might live together in innocence and tranquillity. But just as this training by means of ceremonies was indeed part of their education in the service* of God (in that it made the church of the Jews adhere to God's religion and worship), and yet could nevertheless be distinguished from [the essence of] that service itself, in the same way the [specific] form of their judicial laws is something distinct from the commandment to love, although the sole purpose of these laws was to be the best means of preserving that mutual love which the eternal law of God teaches. And therefore, just as ceremonies could be abrogated without dutifulness* to God being in any way impaired, so judicial laws could be abrogated, and yet leave the perpetual duties and precepts of love intact. And if this is true (FV: and it certainly is), then individual peoples have been left the freedom to make what laws they see to be expedient, but all of these laws must be measured against the law of love. Their form varies, but they must all have the same end. Of course I do not regard as true laws those barbarous and brutish laws by which [for example] robbers were rewarded with honours, or promiscuous intercourse[68] was permitted, and others even more disgusting and absurd; they are abhorrent not only from the point of view of justice but even of humanity.[69]

---

[67] *pedagogia*; the French adds: that is, teaching children. Norton's translation has 'the schooling of the Jews', which is nice.

[68] French version: which permitted intercourse with men and women alike.

[69] The Latin adds: *et mansuetudine*. The French version makes no attempt to say what this might mean, and neither shall I. Norton has 'naturall gentylness and kyndnes of men', whatever that means.

16. My point will become clear if we consider the distinction to be made in any law[70] between the form and content[71] on the one hand, and equity, which is the end for which it is made and the basis on which it rests, on the other. Equity, in as much as it is natural, must be the same for all, and therefore all laws ought to make it their purpose, although accommodated to the particular subject with which they deal. Because positive laws depend in part on specific circumstances, they can [perfectly well] have the same object, namely equity, even though they differ as to their provisions. Now, the Law of God which we call the moral law is acknowledged to be none other than the testimony of natural law and of that conscience which is engraved (FV: imprinted) in the souls of men by God, and so the whole content of equity is prescribed by it. Hence that equity alone must be the end and rule and boundary of all laws. And there is therefore no reason why we should reject any laws whatever, even though they vary amongst themselves or differ from the Mosaic Law, so long as they have equity for the end at which they aim, the rule by reference to which they are formulated, and the limit which they must not transgress. The Law of God forbids theft. What punishments were prescribed for theft in the polity of the Jews may be seen in Exodus. The oldest laws of other nations punished theft by demanding double restitution; later laws distinguished between open and secret theft.[72] Other laws again went as far as exile, whipping and finally the death penalty. Again (FV: the Law of God forbids bearing false witness), the Jews punished false witness by the *lex talionis*,[73] other people punished it by disgrace only, yet others by hanging or crucifixion. (FV: The Law of God forbids murder.) All laws coincide in avenging murder by shedding blood, but they prescribe different forms of death. ⟨Adultery has been punished in some places

---

[70] In the light of the previous sentence, this must mean: anything which can properly be called a law.

[71] Calvin here uses *constitutio*, which means statute or positive law (as opposed to natural and customary law), but it also means: the making of a law, i.e. the act of making, or the precise content, form of words etc. The French word is *ordonnance*, which can also refer both to the act, and to the result of the act, of ordering. He uses the same words *constitutiones/constitutions ou ordonnances*, in the sense of 'positive laws', two sentences further down.

[72] Calvin is here alluding to the Roman-law distinction between *furtum manifestum* and *furtum nec manifestum*; the former was where a culprit was caught in the act, and was for some reason punished more heavily than the latter.

[73] This term is clarified in the French version which (albeit cumbersomely enough) says: false witness was punished by the same penalty that would have been incurred by the person falsely accused, had he been convicted (Deut. 19.19).

by more severe penalties, in others by lighter ones.⟩[74] But for all these variations, we see that in each case the end envisaged is one and the same. For they all with one accord proclaim punishments for those crimes which the eternal Law of God condemns: murder, theft, adultery, false witness; they merely differ as to what the penalty shall be. And it is not necessary or even expedient that they should [all be identical in that respect]. There are regions which would be immediately ravaged by slaughter and brigandage unless a hideous example were made of murderers. There are times which demand increased severity of penalties. [1559:] If the public order (FV: a country) has been disturbed in some way, the evils that commonly arise out of such disturbances must be remedied by new laws. In time of war, amid the clash of arms, all humanity would collapse unless unusual punishments were introduced to inspire fear.[75] In times of dearth or pestilence, everything would go to wrack and ruin, unless greater severity were used. [1536:] Some peoples are particularly prone to certain vices, unless they are held in check by great harshness. And therefore those who object to such diversity, when it is in fact highly suited to maintaining the observance of the Law of God, are malicious enemies of the public good. Nor is there any substance at all in the claim sometimes made, that it is to hold God's Law, as declared by Moses, in contempt to abrogate it and to prefer some new law to it. For when other laws are found more acceptable, it is not a question of an [unconditional] preference, but rather of reference to the conditions of time, place and people. Nor can it be called 'abrogating the Law of Moses', when it was never decreed for us in the first place. The Lord did not have Moses promulgate the Law for all peoples and all times. Rather, his will was to be the [sole and] special lawgiver for the Jewish people, whom he had taken under his patronage and protection, and made his clients.[76] And so, in the manner of a good lawgiver, he had regard in all his laws to [the special needs of] this people.

---

[74] The omission of this sentence from the French version may be mere inadvertence, rather than a judgement on Calvin's part about the sensibilities of his French readers; the next sentence in both French and Latin versions includes adultery among the crimes condemned by both divine and human law.

[75] French version: in time of war all humanity would be forgotten, if the reins were not held more tightly, and excesses punished [more severely].

[76] The analogy is that of the Roman patron–client system, where some powerful person took persons of lower standing under his protection, in return for their services and dependency.

17. It remains for us to consider the topic we proposed to deal with last, namely what benefits accrue to the ⟨general⟩ association of Christians from laws, courts and magistrates. And to this is attached another question, namely how far the obedience and submission which private men owe to magistrates [FV: superiors] extends. Many regard the office of magistrate as irrelevant as far as Christians are concerned. They claim that Christians are not entitled to appeal to magistrates for help, since all vengeance, all appeals to courts and all litigation are prohibited [by God]. But on the contrary, as St Paul plainly declares (Rom. 13.4), [magistrates] are ministers[77] of God for our good. This teaches us that it has been divinely ordained that we should be defended by the hand and protection of the magistrate against the outrages and injustices of the wicked, and so be able to live our lives in peace and safety. God would have accorded us such protection in vain, if we were forbidden to make use of it, and so it is evident enough that we can call on it without any sin. But here I have two sorts of people to contend with.[78] There are many whose passion for litigation is so all-consuming that they can never be at peace with themselves unless they are at war with others. They embark on lawsuits in a spirit of mortal hatred and bitterness, with an insane thirst for revenge and for inflicting suffering, and they pursue their suits with implacable persistency until their adversary is ruined. And all the while, they defend their wickedness with the pretext of legality, so that no one will think of them as doing anything except what is right. But even though it is legitimate to take one's brother to court,[79] it does not follow that it is right to hate him, to be possessed by a rage to do him harm, or to hound him relentlessly (FV adds: without mercy).

18. Let such men learn this (FV: maxim): making use of courts is legitimate if one uses them rightly. And the right way to use them is this: the accused, on being summoned, should appear on the appointed day, and defend his cause by producing what justification he can, without bitterness, and with no other intention but that of safeguarding what is his by right. The plaintiff who has been made to suffer unjustly either in respect of his person or his goods, should put himself in the hands of the magistrate, should explain the charge he has brought and ask for

---

[77] See fn. 25 above.
[78] The second sort is not mentioned until section 19.
[79] French version: just because a man is allowed to compel his neighbour to do right by the verdict [of a court] . . .

what is just and right. But he should do all this without any thirst for revenge or desire to inflict injury, without bitterness or hate, and without taking pleasure in quarrelsomeness; on the contrary, he should be prepared to yield up his right and suffer any wrong rather than to allow his mind to be filled with enmity towards his adversary. On the other hand, where any particle of [the duty to] love is neglected because minds are suffused with ill-will, corrupted by envy, burning with anger, breathing vengeance, or inflamed by quarrelsomeness, then every legal proceeding must be contrary to our duties* to God, however just it might be in itself. It ought to be considered a principle laid down for every Christian that it is impossible for anyone to proceed justly with a case at law, however good his cause, unless he bears towards his adversary the same love and benevolence [that he would] if the business at issue had already been amicably transacted and settled. Some will perhaps object here that such (FV: moderation and) self-restraint is never in fact to be found in the lawcourts, and that it would be a miracle if ever one saw an instance of it. I admit that, the morals of our times being what they are, one rarely encounters an instance of a virtuous litigant, but the thing itself does not cease to be good and pure, provided it remains untainted by evil. And when we hear that the assistance which the magistrate renders is a sacred gift of God, we must take all the more care not to sully it by our viciousness.

19.   As for those who condemn all courts and all litigation absolutely and without distinction, they should realize that they are rejecting a sacred ordinance of God and one of those [divine] gifts which can be pure to those who are pure. Unless, that is, they want to charge St Paul [himself] with a crime. For he rebutted the calumnies of his accusers, exposing their craftiness and malice into the bargain, asserted his privileges as a Roman citizen in the courts, and appealed from a wicked judge to the tribunal of Caesar when the need arose (Acts 22.1, 24.12, 25.10). Nor is the fact that all Christians are forbidden to desire vengeance any objection: we too would have such desires banished from Christian courts (Matt. 5.39; Deut. 32.35; Rom. 12.19). For if the matter is a civil one, there is no right way except that of commending one's case to the judge, as guardian of the public [good], in innocent simplicity and without the least thought of returning evil for evil (that is, without any desire for vengeance); or if it is a more serious or capital case that is to be brought before a court, we require of an accuser that he should not be animated by a thirst for revenge, that his mind should

be untouched by rancour for the injustice he has suffered, and that his only intention should be to impede wicked men in their endeavour to damage the commonwealth. For if there is no vengeful intent, there is nothing in all this that goes against the commandment that Christians should not avenge themselves. But here [the rejoinder might be that] Christians are not only forbidden to avenge themselves, they are also commanded to wait for the hand of God, who has promised to avenge the oppressed and afflicted. And those who call on magistrates to help them or others, forestall the celestial vengeance of their divine protector. But that objection [too] is quite groundless: the magistrate's punishment must be regarded as something inflicted by God, not by men, for it is God who acts in this way for our good by means of the ministry[80] of men, as St Paul says (Rom. 13.4).

20.   Nor is there any contradiction between what we teach here and the saying of Christ (Matt. 5.39) which forbids us to resist evil and commands us to turn the right cheek to the person who strikes us on the left, and to allow him who takes our tunic to take our cloak as well. Christ does indeed demand of his followers that any thought of revenge should be so far from their minds that they would rather suffer twice the harm inflicted on them than to retaliate. But we are not discouraging such patience. Christians must be people born to suffer contumely and injustices, and to be exposed to wickedness, deceit and ridicule from the dregs of mankind. And not only this, but they must bear all such evils patiently, that is, with such composure that when they suffer one affliction, they should prepare themselves for more to come, expecting nothing throughout the whole of their lives except a perpetual carrying of their cross. In the mean time, they must do good to those who harm them and pray for those who speak evil against them, and they must seek to overcome evil with good, for this is to be their only victory (Rom. 12.21; Matt. 5.39). If this is how they are disposed, they will not demand an eye for an eye or a tooth for a tooth, seeking revenge, which is what the Pharisees taught their disciples. Rather, following Christ's injunction, they will allow their bodies to be mutilated and their goods to be maliciously seized, and yet be ready to forgive the injuries they suffer the very moment they are inflicted. But this equitableness and composure of mind will not inhibit them from making use of the help of magistrates for the preservation of what is

---

[80] See fn. 25 above.

to Titus (3.1): 'Exhort them to be subject to principalities and powers; they should obey the magistrates and be ready for every good work.' And Peter says (1 Pet. 2.13): 'Be subject to every human creature ⟨[1545:] (or rather, as I interpret it, every human ordinance)⟩ [1536:] for God's sake, whether it be the king as having pre-eminence, or governors, who are sent by him to punish the wicked, but to give praise to those who act rightly.' What is more, in order to prove that their subjection is not merely feigned subjection, but rather that it is sincere and comes from the heart, Paul adds (1 Tim. 2.1) that subjects are to pray for the well-being and prosperity of those under whom they live. 'I exhort you', he says, 'to offer prayers, petitions and thanksgiving for all men, for kings and for all placed in authority, that we may live peaceful and quiet lives in all godliness and decency.' And make no mistake: it is impossible to resist the magistrate without also resisting God. Even if it appears possible to defy an unarmed magistrate with impunity, God is armed and his vengeance for any contempt shown him is harsh. The obedience [of which I am speaking] also includes that self-restraint which private persons ought to impose on themselves in public [matters], neither meddling in public matters, nor intruding rashly on the magistrate's preserve, nor undertaking anything whatever of a public nature. If there is something in need of correction in the public order*, private men are not to create disturbances, or take matters into their own hands, for these hands ought here to be tied. Instead, they should submit the matter to the cognizance of the magistrate (FV: superior), whose hand alone is free. What I mean is that they should do nothing, unless they have a specific right or command to do so.[84] For where a superior lends them his authority,[85] then they too are invested with public authority. The ruler's advisers are commonly described as his 'eyes and ears'; it would not be inappropriate to call those whom he has commissioned to act for him his 'hands'.

24.   Up to this point we have been considering[86] magistrates who live up to the titles given to them: fathers of their country, or ⟨as the poet[87] puts it⟩ shepherds of the people, guardians of the peace, upholders of

---

[84] This whole clause translates one word: *iniussi*.

[85] French version: for where a superior's command is given them ... *Imperium* sometimes means a command, so this might be what the Latin means. It is what Norton thought it meant.

[86] Both the French and the Latin say 'describing', but Calvin has not, of course, been describing anything.

[87] i.e. Homer.

justice, defenders of the innocent. And anyone who thinks the authority of such persons unacceptable deserves to be considered a madman. But we find in almost every age another sort of prince.[88] Some of them live lives of indolence and pleasure, not in the least concerned about all those duties to which they ought to attend. Others, intent only on their own profit, prostitute every right, privilege, judgement and charter by putting them up for sale. Others again drain the poor people of their money, only to squander it in wild prodigality. Yet others pillage homes, violate wives and maidens, slaughter the innocent; in short, they engage in what can only be called criminality. And there are many people who cannot be convinced that these too ought to be acknowledged as princes, and ⟨as being endowed with an authority* which is⟩ to be obeyed, as far as is permissible. For they cannot see any semblance of that image of God which ought to shine forth from magistrates, nor any vestige of that 'minister of God' who is given to the righteous in praise and to the wicked for their punishment. Faced with such lack of dignity and with criminal conduct so remote from the duties of a magistrate, indeed so remote from the duties of ordinary humanity, they cannot recognize the kind of superior whose dignity and authority Scripture commends to us. Mankind has always had an innate hatred and detestation of tyrants, just as it loves and venerates lawful[89] kings.

25.   But reflection on the Word of God will carry us beyond [the ordinary sentiments of mankind]. For we are to be subject not only to the authority* of those princes who do their duty towards us as they should, and uprightly, but to all of them, however they came by their office, even if the very last thing they do is to act like [true] princes. For even though the Lord declares that the [office of] magistrate is the greatest gift of his goodness for the preservation of mankind, and although he himself sets the boundaries within which they are to confine themselves, nonetheless he also declares at the same time that whatever they are (FV: and however they govern), it is from him alone that they derive their authority. Those who govern for the public good are true examples (FV: mirrors) and signs of his goodness; those who govern unjustly and intemperately have been raised up by him to

---

[88] I do not know whether the antithesis between 'prince' here and 'magistrate' in the first sentence of this section is deliberate.

[89] My translation equivocates: *legitimos* means legitimate, lawful, but this makes no sense except if it means: who govern according to law. The French version more sensibly has: just kings, and those who truly acquit themselves of their duty.

punish the iniquity of the people. Both are equally furnished with that sacred majesty, with which he has endowed legitimate authority (FV: superiors). I shall not continue without offering some proof-texts for my point: Job 34.30; Hosea 13.11; Isaiah 3.4 and 10.5; Deuteronomy 28.29. We need not devote much effort to proving that an ungodly king is the wrath of God on the land; there is no one (I imagine) who will deny it, and in any case this says no more about kings than might equally be said of a robber who steals your goods, or an adulterer who defiles your marriage-bed, or a murderer who encompasses your death; all these calamities are counted by Scripture amongst God's curses (Deut. 28.29). What however does require more proof, because people are much less ready to accept it, is that even the worst of them, and those entirely undeserving of any honour, provided they have public authority, are invested with that splendid and sacred authority which God's Word bestows on the ministers[90] of his justice and judgement. And hence, as far as public obedience is concerned, they are to be held in the same honour and reverence as would be accorded an excellent king, if they had such a one.

26.   So that in the first place I would have my readers note and meditate on this: it is not without good reason that Scripture so often reminds us of God's providence and his special operation[91] in distributing kingdoms and setting up such kings as he sees fit. As it says in Daniel (2.21 and 37): 'The Lord changes the times and the diversity of times; he overthrows kings and sets them up.' And again: 'Let the living know that the Most High is mighty in the kingdom of men and gives [the kingship] to whomever he wishes.' The whole of Scripture abounds in such passages, but they are especially frequent in the prophets. Everyone knows what sort of a king Nebuchadnezzar was, the man who took Jerusalem and who was always bent on invading and ravaging other men's lands.[92] And yet in Ezekiel (29.19) the Lord affirms that it was He himself who gave him the land of Egypt, in return for the service he had rendered Him in laying it waste. And Daniel said to him (Ezek. 2.37): 'You O King are the king of kings, to whom the Lord of heaven has given a kingdom powerful, strong and glorious; to

---

[90] See fn. 25 above.

[91] *actio*; I have used the term from the French version. The reference is to Calvin's distinction between the 'general' providence of God, by which all things operate of themselves according to his will, and his 'special providences' (as godly Englishmen termed it), where God intervenes directly on behalf of his servants.

[92] French version: a great robber and pillager.

you I say he gave it, and all the lands inhabited by the sons of men, the beasts of the forest (FV: wild beasts) and the birds of the air; he gave them into your hand and made you to rule over them.' And again to his son Belshazzar (Dan. 5.18): 'The Lord the Most High gave to your father Nebuchadnezzar kingship and magnificence, honour and glory; and on account of the greatness he conferred on him, all peoples, tribes and tongues were fearful and trembled in his sight.' When we hear that God established such a king, we must also recall to mind the divine ordinances about honouring and fearing kings, nor must we be in any doubt that we must honour [even] the worst tyrant in the office in which the Lord has seen fit to set him. When Samuel proclaimed to the people of Israel what they would have to endure from their kings, he said (1 Sam. 8.11): 'This will be the right (*ius*) of the king who will reign over you: he will take your sons and put them to his chariots to be his horsemen, to work his fields and gather in his harvest, and to make him weapons. He will take your daughters to make perfumes, to cook and to bake. He will take your fields and your vineyards and your best olive-groves and give them to his servants. He will take tithes of your seed and your grape-harvest and give them to his eunuchs and servants. He will take your servants, handmaidens and asses and apply them to his work and will take tithes of your flocks besides, and you shall be his servants.' Kings will not indeed do all this by right;[93] on the contrary, God's law fully instructs them in temperance and self-restraint. But Samuel calls it a right (*ius*) over the people, because they must obey the king and are not allowed to resist him. It is as if Samuel had said: kings will be carried away by their licentiousness, but it will not be for you to restrain them; all that will remain for you will be to hear what they command, and obey.

27. One passage stands out as especially important and memorable: Jeremiah 27.5ff. I am prepared to quote it because, although it is somewhat long, it resolves the question in the clearest possible fashion. [It reads:] 'The Lord says: I have made heaven, and mankind, and the

---

[93] French version: justly. The Latin is *iure*, by right. This passage is the *locus classicus* for absolutist interpretations of kingship. Calvin wanted no truck with any 'absolute' authority except that of God, but he apparently read the Scriptural text as containing in vs. 11 a reference to 'the right' (*ius*) of kings, although no pre-modern language has any such concept. (Cf. R. Tuck, *Natural Rights Theories: Their Origin and Development* (Cambridge: Cambridge University Press, 1979). He had therefore to attenuate. The French version simply eliminates the difficulty, by means of the ambiguous word *puissance*, which means either might or power. See Glossary: authority.

animals who are on the surface of the earth, in the greatness of my power and by my outstretched arm, and have handed them over to whoever is pleasing in my sight. And now therefore I have given all these lands into the hands of my servant Nebuchadnezzar; let all the peoples and the ⟨great⟩ kings serve him until the time of his land shall come. And it shall come to pass that every people and kingdom which has not served the king of Babel (FV: and has not bowed the neck under his yoke), I shall visit that people with sword, hunger and pestilence; therefore serve the king of Babel and live.' We see here the degree of obedience and honour the Lord wished to be accorded to that loathsome and cruel tyrant, and merely because he was in possession of the kingship. It was this [possession] alone which showed that he had been placed on the royal throne by divine decree, and had been vested with royal majesty, which must remain inviolate. If we keep firmly in mind that even the very worst kings are appointed by this same decree which establishes the authority of kings [in general], then we will never permit ourselves the seditious idea that a king is to be treated according to his deserts, or that we need not obey a king who does not conduct himself towards us like a king.

28.   There is no force either in the objection that this precept was exclusively for the Israelites. We must consider the reason God himself gave to support it. What he says is: 'I have given the kingdom to Nebuchadnezzar; therefore serve him and live' (Jer. 27.17). Thus we cannot doubt that we must serve anyone who has manifestly had kingship conferred on him. In the very act of raising someone to the exalted rank of king, the Lord thereby reveals to us that it is his will that that person should rule. And there are general testimonies to the truth of this to be found in Scripture. In Solomon (Prov. 28.1): 'Because of the iniquity of the land there are many princes.'[94] And Job 12.18: 'He takes away dominion from princes, and then girds them again with a girdle.'[95] When that is admitted, there remains nothing for us but to serve and live. And in the Prophet Jeremiah (29.7) we find another command of the Lord. There he orders his people to seek peace in Babylon, to which they had been taken by force as captives, and to pray to him for Babylon, for in its peace would be their peace. Notice how the Israelites, despoiled of all their goods, expelled from their homes, carried off into exile, cast down into a wretched bondage, are [yet]

---

[94] French version: there are many changes of princes.
[95] French version: exalts them in power.

commanded to pray for the prosperity of their conqueror. And not merely in the sense that we are elsewhere commanded to pray for those who persecute us, but rather, to pray for the peace and safety of his reign, so that they too might live prosperously under him. And in the same way David, already designated king by God's ordinance and anointed with his holy oil, when he was persecuted by Saul without having done anything to deserve it, nonetheless treated the person of his ambusher as sacrosanct, because God had honoured Saul with the royal dignity. 'Far be it from me,' he said (1 Sam. 24.6 and 11),'that I should do this thing to my lord, the Anointed of the Lord, in the sight of the Lord my God: that I should lay my hands on him (FV: to do him harm); for he is (FV: the Christ, that is,) the Lord's Anointed.' And again (1 Sam. 26.9): 'My soul has spared you and I have said: I shall not lay hands on my lord, since he is the Anointed of the Lord.' And again: 'Who shall lay hands on the Anointed of the Lord and remain guiltless? The Lord lives, and unless the Lord strikes him down, or his day comes and he dies, or is laid low in battle, far be it from me that I should lay hands on the Anointed of the Lord' (1 Sam. 24.7–11; 26.9 and 10).

29. This is the kind of reverence and dutifulness* that we all owe to our superiors,[96] whoever they are. I say this often, so that we might learn not to consider the persons and conduct [of rulers], but be content with the person they represent, by the will of God, and with ⟨whose⟩ inviolable majesty ⟨they have been inscribed and stamped⟩.[97] But, you will reply, superiors in their turn reciprocally owe duties to their subjects. I have already acknowledged it. But if you go on to infer that only just governments (FV: just lords) are to be repaid by obedience, your reasoning is stupid. Husbands and wives owe each other mutual duties; so do parents and children. But what if husbands or parents do not do their duty? What if parents, although forbidden to provoke their children to anger (Eph. 6.4), are instead hard and intractable and weary their children beyond measure by their peevishness?[98] What if husbands treat their wives with great abusiveness, even though they have been commanded to love and spare them, as weak vessels (Eph. 5.25; 1 Pet. 3.7)? Shall children then be less obedient to

---

[96] French version adds: which we see in David.

[97] The French version reads: in order that we might learn not to examine minutely who are the persons whom we have to obey, but that we should rest content with the knowledge that it is the will of the Lord that they have been established in a position (*estat*) to which he has given an inviolable majesty.

[98] *morositas*; one of Calvin's favourite words, the meaning of which is somewhat obscure.

their parents, or wives to their husbands on that account? But [children and wives] are subject to the wicked and the undutiful just as much [as to the upright and dutiful]. No: all are to act in such a way as not to look at the bag hanging from the backs of other people;[99] that is, they are not to ask about the duties of others, but only to consider their own, and especially when they are placed in subjection to the power of others. Hence, if we are tormented by a cruel ruler, if we are fleeced by a rapacious and extravagant one, if we suffer neglect from an indolent one or are afflicted for [our] godliness by an impious and sacrilegious one, let us first recall to mind our sins, for it is those without a doubt which God is punishing by such scourges. Then humility will bridle our impatience. And let us all summon this reflection to our assistance: it is not for us to remedy such evils; all that is left to us is to implore the help of the Lord, for the hearts of princes and alterations of kingdoms are in his hands (Prov. 21.1). It is God who will stand in the assembly of the gods and will give judgement in their midst (Ps. 82.1). Before his face all kings will fall down and be terrified, and the judges who had not kissed his Anointed (Ps. 2.12); those who wrote unjust laws to oppress the poor by their judgements and to do violence to the cause of the humble; to prey on widows and rob orphans (Isa. 10.1–2).

30.   And in all this is revealed God's admirable goodness, might and providence. For sometimes he raises up avengers from amongst his servants, designated and commanded by him to punish the tyranny of vicious men[100] and to deliver the oppressed from their wretched calamities; at other times he turns the frenzy of men who intended something quite different to the same end. In the former manner[101] he freed the people of Israel from Pharaoh's tyranny by means of Moses, from the violence of Chusan, King of Syria, by Othoniel, and from other servitudes by other kings or judges (Exod. 3.8; Judg. 3.9 and ff chs.). And by the latter means he overcame the pride of Tyre by means of the Egyptians, the haughtiness of the Egyptians by the Assyrians, the ferocity of the Assyrians by the Chaldeans, the overweening pride of Babylon by the Medes and Persians, when Cyrus had already subjugated the Medes. On occasion, he punished the ingratitude shown him by the kings of Israel and Judah for his many mercies, and their

---

[99] This lively metaphor for once only occurs in the Latin and not the French version.
[100] This is my attempt to render *de scelerata dominatione*.
[101] This is from the French version; the Latin merely has: thus.

contempt to him, by means of the Assyrians, on other occasions by the Babylonians, though in quite different ways. The former [i.e. the avengers] were summoned to punish these crimes by a lawful calling from God; they did not in the least violate the majesty with which kings are endowed by divine ordinance when they took up arms against kings. Armed by heaven, they subjugated a lesser power* by a greater, in just the same way that kings are entitled to punish their own officials. The latter, by contrast, did God's work without knowing it, for all that they intended to do was to commit crimes. All the same, it was the hand of God that directed them do to his bidding.

31. But irrespective of what may be thought about the actions them-selves,[102] it was the Lord who by these instruments carried out his just purpose, when he broke the bloodstained sceptres of insolent kings and overturned unbearable tyrannies.[103] Let princes hear and be afraid. As for us, however, let us take the greatest possible care never to hold in contempt, or trespass upon, that plenitude of authority* of magistrates (FV: superiors) whose majesty it is for us to venerate and which God has confirmed by the most weighty pronouncements, even when it is exercised by individuals who are wholly unworthy of it and who do their best to defile it by their wickedness. And even if the punishment of unbridled tyranny is the Lord's vengeance [on tyrants], we are not to imagine that it is we ourselves who have been called upon to inflict it. All that has been assigned to us is to obey and suffer. Here as always, I am speaking about private persons. It may be that there are in our days popular magistrates[104] established to restrain the licentiousness of kings, corresponding to those 'Ephors' (FV: as they were called), which were set against the authority of the kings of the Spartans, or the Tribunes (FV: defenders) of the People, set over against the Roman consuls,[105] or the 'Demarchs', set up against the Council of the

---

[102] French version: However, although these actions were quite different, in respect of those who did them, for the former acted in sure knowledge that they were doing what was right, the others with quite a different object...

[103] *Dominationes/dominations*; see Glossary: authority.

[104] The French omits 'popular', and reads: magistrates established to defend the people, to restrain the excessive greed and licence of kings... The difference in vocabulary is of considerable significance, in that the Latin *populares* was a term quite different in connotation from 'inferior' or 'lesser', the more usual Lutheran terms in this context. Cf. Skinner, *Foundations* (Cambridge: Cambridge University Press, 1978), vol. II, pp. 230–4.

[105] The French version reads simply: the Romans [had] their defenders of the people (*defenseurs populaires*)...

Athenians.[106] And perhaps, in current circumstances, the authority exercised by the three estates in individual kingdoms when they hold their principal assemblies is of the same kind. If there are such [popular magistrates established], then it is no part of my intention to prohibit them from acting in accordance with their duty, and resisting the licentiousness and frenzy of kings; on the contrary, if they connive at their unbridled violence and insults against the poor common people, I say that such negligence is a nefarious betrayal of their oath; they are betraying the people and defrauding them of that liberty which they know they were ordained by God to defend.

32. But there is always one exception to that obedience which, as we have established, is due to ⟨the authority of⟩ superiors, and it is this that must be our principal concern:[107] we must never allow ourselves to be diverted from our obedience to the one to whose will the desires of every king must be subjected, to whose decrees all their commands give place, and before whose majesty they must lay down their own insignia.[108] Would it not be an absurdity to give contentment to [mere] men [by obeying them], but thereby to incur the wrath of him on whose account alone [any human being at all] must be obeyed? The Lord is the king of kings. When his sacred mouth has spoken, it alone and no one else is to be heard. We are subject to those who have been placed over us, but only in him. If they command anything against [his will], it must be as nothing to us. And in this instance we must ignore all that dignity that magistrates (FV: superiors) possess. There is no injustice in compelling it to be subordinate to the true, unique and supreme power[109] of God. [1559:] It is for this reason that Daniel (Dan. 6.22) denied that he was guilty of any offence against the king when he disobeyed an ungodly law the latter had made: for the king had transgressed the bounds set to him [by God] and had not only wronged men, but had raised his horns against God, thereby abrogating his own

---

[106] The French version reads: the Athenians [had] their Demarchs. Calvin's Latin term 'the Senate' is his usual word for a governing council, but seems singularly inappropriate here.

[107] French version: a rule to be kept which overrides everything else;

[108] Literally *fasces*, the axes carried before Roman chief magistrates as a symbol of the power of life and death.

[109] *Summa potestas*, which like *plena autoritas* in s. 31, is a possible early modern way of rendering 'sovereignty'. The French version simply reads: under the power (*puissance*) of God, which is the only true [power], at the expense of all the others.

power.[110] By contrast, the Israelites are condemned (FV: in Hosea 5.11) for their excessive readiness to submit to an ungodly law of their king. For when Jeroboam had had the golden calves cast, they defected from the temple of God and went over to new superstitions (1 Kings 12.30), in order to please him. Their descendants were just as ready to accommodate themselves to the will and pleasure of their kings. They too were sharply reproved by the prophet for submitting to the king's commands. Thus there is nothing at all to praise in that pretended 'humble submission' which the flatterers at court[111] invoke to cover themselves and deceive the simple, when they claim that it is wrong for them to refuse obedience to anything their kings command. As if God had surrendered his own rights to the mortal men he has placed in authority over the human race. Or as if earthly power suffered diminution by being subjected to God's, who is its author and in whose sight even the celestial principalities tremble in fear ⟨and supplication⟩. [1536:] I recognize full well the gravity and the immediacy of the perils which threaten [those who show] the constancy I demand; I know that kings are not prepared to tolerate any defiance and that their anger is a messenger of death, as Solomon says (Prov. 16.14). But heaven's messenger Peter (in Acts 5.29) proclaims this commandment: 'We must obey God rather than men.' Let us therefore derive consolation from the thought that we are rendering to God the obedience he demands when we rather suffer all things than to depart from our duty* to him.[112] And so that our courage may not fail us, Paul (1 Cor. 7, 23) adduces something else to spur us on: our redemption has been purchased at so high a price in order that we might not become slaves to the wicked desires of men; still less should we submit to their ungodliness*.

PRAISE BE TO GOD

---

[110] The implication of this, which Calvin did not pursue, is that any ruler who sets himself against God, *ipso facto* ceases to be a ruler. This is not what Calvin intended, for the rest of his argument would be nullified by such an admission. It is, however, precisely what some of his successors meant.

[111] See section 1.

[112] The French version reads: depart from his Holy Word.

Addendum: translation of the French version of section 8

[1536:] And indeed it is an idle occupation for private men, who have no right (*authorité*) to order republics [or public affairs: *ordonner les choses publiques*] to debate the question about the best order of a polity (*estat de police*). Besides, it is an act of rashness to claim to have an unconditional answer to this question, seeing that it depends principally on circumstances. And again, [even] if one did compare [forms of] polities without regard to circumstances, it would not be easy to decide which is the most beneficial, so equal are they in their respective worth. [1541:][113] People reckon three forms of civil government: monarchy, which is government (*domination*) by a single individual, whether his title is king, duke or whatever; aristocracy, which is a form of government (*domination*) in which the leading men, men of standing, govern; and democracy, which is popular government, that is, each member of the people has power (*puissance*). [1536:] Now it is certainly true that a king, or anyone else who holds supreme power (*domination*), easily degenerates into a tyrant. But equally, when men of standing [in the community] have supremacy, it is just as easy for them to establish an iniquitous tyranny (*domination inique*). And when the populace has authority, it is easier still for it to become turbulent and seditious. [1543:] It is indeed true that if one compares the three forms of government I listed, it is government by those of standing in the community,[114] provided they preserve the people's freedom, which ought to be rated as the best [form], [1560:] not so much in and for itself, but because it is a rare event – in fact it is almost a miracle when it does happen – for kings to keep themselves so well under control that their will never departs from what is right and equitable. And besides, it is rare for kings to be furnished with such prudence and sharpness of mind that they [always] recognize what is good and useful. And so it is because of the vices or defects of human beings that the most tolerable and reliable form of government is for several persons to govern [jointly], each helping the others and recalling them to their duty; so that if one of them raises himself too high, the others may act as his censors and masters [or teachers: *maîtres*]. [1543:] Experience has

---

[113] The following sentence occurs only in the French; presumably Calvin regarded it as too elementary to warrant inclusion in the Latin version (intended for the more literate public), and so it was: elementary, cursory, and totally derivative.

[114] I think this is the meaning of the peculiar expression *la pre-eminence de ceux qui gouvernent*.

always shown this [to be so], and God has in any case confirmed it by his authority when he ordained that this [form of government] should be the one to which the people of Israel should be subject, from the time when he wanted to keep it in the best condition possible [1559:] until he established an image of our Lord Jesus in David.[115] [1543:] And indeed since the best sort of government is one which permits a well-tempered liberty, and one designed to last, I readily admit that those who are allowed to enjoy such a condition are fortunate (*bien-heureux*), and I say that they are doing no more than their duty if they are constantly occupied in preserving it. And the governors of a free people ought to employ all their efforts in seeing to it that the people's freedom, whose protectors they are, suffers no diminution of any sort under their rule. And I also say that if they are careless and indifferent about preserving it, or if they allow it to fall into decay, they are disloyal and traitors. But if those who by the will of God live under princes, and are their natural subjects,[116] treat what I have said as applying to them,[117] and are thereby tempted to bring about some rebellion or change, it will not be merely a stupid and pointless speculation but a wicked and pernicious one. [1541:]

[At this point the text resumes its approximation to the Latin.]

[115]   This sentence, which seems to me as mystifying in the French as it is in the Latin, ought perhaps to be read in conjunction with the previous section's point about Scripture specifically setting out to overturn merely human judgements against monarchy. Although Calvin never altered his view that where monarchy was established, it was as legitimate and irremovable a form of government as any other, he had equally by 1543 come himself to hold pronouncedly anti-monarchical attitudes, qualified only by his disposition to regard facticity in political matters as providential, and by his conviction that the Israelitic kingdom of David was itself a providential dispensation, not a merely human vagary.

[116]   This phrase 'natural subjects' occurs only in the French, and must be intended specifically for Calvin's French disciples, whom he was constantly trying to prevent from engaging in outright rebellion.

[117]   That at any rate is my interpretation of Calvin's devastatingly casual '*S'ils transferent cela à eux…*'

Index

Index

Mullett, M., xlvi

Norton, Thomas, xxv and fn. 9, 67 and
    fns. 67 and 69, 75 and fn. 85

Obedience
    Christian duty of, in **Luther**: xiv, 14,
        28, 29 and fn. 41, 40 (in war)
    limits of duty, in matters of faith, 22ff,
        29; in unjust wars, 40
    in **Calvin**: xvi–xvii, xviii, 57, 74, 76–81
        and fn. 97 (irrespective of conduct
        and titles of rulers)
    duties of public and private persons
        distinguished, xviii, 55–7 and fn. 30,
        82
    limits of duty of obedience, 69, 83–4
Oberen, Oberkeit, see Superiors
Office *see* Duty
Old Testament, Old Covenant
    OT and NT teachings on secular
        authority compatible:
    according to **Luther**: 7, 8, 16–17, 18,
        20, 21, 39 fn. 56
    according to **Calvin**: 52–3, 63, 66–7,
        68–9
Oresko, R., xlvi
Ozment, S., xliv

Papacy
    Luther on, viii, 4
    compared to 'Leviathan', 6 and fn. 8
    pope as 'idol' of princes, 6, 25, 29
    proper role of, 26 and fn. 36
    cites scriptural *loci classici* for papal
        authority, 23 and fn. 29
    no authority over soul, 24–5
Parker, T. H. L., xlvi
Peace
    Luther: imposed on the unchristian by
        secular government, 11, 12, 13, 14;
        one of ends of government, 15, 38–
        9, 40; war and p., 39
    Calvin: war as search for peace, 64; as
        an end of civil government, 49, 50,
        59
1 Peter 2
    cited by **Luther**, 6, 13, 27, 28
    cited by **Calvin**, 55, 74, 75
pietas see Just, Godliness
Plato, cited by Calvin, 65
potestas see Authority

police see Polity
Polity, Civil Order, Commonwealth
    Luther's terminology: *Reich*, xxxvi;
        Gemeinde, x, xli–xlii, 22 and fn. 26
    Calvin's terminology: *politia/police*, xx–
        xxi, xlii, 48 fn. 3; *respublica/
        république*, xlii
    all polities established by God, 48, 49
    benefits from, 50
    duties include care of religion,
        prevention of blasphemy and
        sacrilege, 50
    forms of p., forms of government, 56–
        7, 85–6; mixed form the best, 65–7,
        85; specific form of government in
        any p. assigned by Providence, 57
    free commonwealth, 57
    laws and the p., 65, *see* Law
    p. of the Jews, 67
    rewards and punishments necessary in
        any p., 59
    specialized sense of term p.,
        distinguished from democracy, 56–7
        and fns. 31 and 33, 85
Popular Magistrates *see* Magistrates
Power, Force, Violence
    Luther's terminology: *Gewalt, Oberkeit*,
        xv–xvi, xxxvii; *Gewalt* as synonym for
        Oberkeit (secular authority, rulers),
        xiv–xvi, 6, 14, 21, 25, 28; as meaning
        force, violence (contrasted with law,
        right *qv*), 29, 30, 31 and fn. 43, 33,
        34, 39 and fn. 56
    Christ did not exercise p., 18–20
    force useless against heresy, 30–1
    priestly office not one of superiority or
        p., 33
    See also Sword
    Calvin's terminology: *potestas/
        puissance, dominatio/domination*,
        xxxviii, xl; *potentia*, 48 and fn. 4
    power of God (*summa potestas*), 83 and
        fn. 109; plenitude of (*plenitudo*), 82
praefectus, praefectura see Superiors
Princes, Kings, Emperors
    Luther's terminology: xiv, xxv–xxxvi;
        translates *principes* as *Fürsten*
        (princes), 32
    as bad as the spiritual tyrants, 27; act as
        if they were bishops, 30, 32
    common man's growing hostility to, 32,
        33 and fn. 45, 36–7; and their

92

Cambridge Texts in the History of Political Thought

Titles published in the series thus far

Aristotle *The Politics* (edited by Stephen Everson)

Bakunin *Statism and Anarchy* (edited by Marshall Shatz)

Bentham *A Fragment on Government* (introduction by Ross Harrison)

Bossuet *Politics drawn from the Very Words of Holy Scripture* (edited by Patrick Riley)

Cicero *On Duties* (edited by M. T. Griffin and E. M. Atkins)

Constant *Political Writings* (edited by Biancamaria Fontana)

Filmer *Patriarcha and Other Writings* (edited by Johann P. Sommerville)

Hobbes *Leviathan* (edited by Richard Tuck)

Hooker *Of the Laws of Ecclesiastical Polity* (edited by A. S. McGrade)

John of Salisbury *Policraticus* (edited by Cary Nederman)

Kant *Political Writings* (edited by H. S. Reiss and H. B. Nisbet)

Leibniz *Political Writings* (edited by Patrick Riley)

Locke *Two Treatises of Government* (edited by Peter Laslett)

Luther and Calvin on Secular Authority (edited by Harro Höpfl)

Machiavelli *The Prince* (edited by Quentin Skinner and Russell Price)

J. S. Mill *On Liberty* with *The Subjection of Women* and *Chapters on Socialism* (edited by Stefan Collini)

Milton *Political Writings* (edited by Martin Dzelzainis)

Montesquieu *The Spirit of the Laws* (edited by Anne M. Cohler, Basia Carolyn Miller and Harold Samuel Stone)

More *Utopia* (edited by George M. Logan and Robert M. Adams)

Paine *Political Writings* (edited by Bruce Kuklick)